This book is a result of a lifetime of engagement and collaboration as father and son. While we have each pursued very different paths - each blessed though not always fully understood by the other – we have remained united in a shared passion for the Kingdom of God, here on earth, as it is in heaven. As a cell surrounds its nucleus, the letters here were penned by Chris around the vision of Jim, as a son sought to give words to the deep desires and faith of a father now diminished in some capacity through age, but nonetheless vibrant and intensely alive and full of a deep desire to still pour encouragement into the lives of his many friends.

Each week, Chris gathered notes from Jim, sometimes written, sometimes through conversations and sometimes with just a few words of an emerging theme. Often, "what are you thinking about now, Dad?" would prompt a new vector, or the start of a new idea, often prompted by hymns whose words offered Chris the clues he needed to frame the letter. For a son, it was both all new and all so familiar – his father's heart ever beating in such familiar ways, always yearning to encourage others, and just occasionally moderated and grounded by wife of Jim and mother of Chris, Rita, who perhaps still, as always, insists on the 'last word'!

We think that this is the finest literary fruit we have ever borne together, and it took most of two life-times to accomplish! Through it we grew closer together, understood each other more deeply and both received encouragement as our shared work was received by others.

Jim & Chris Houston
January 2024

Letters from a Hospital Bed

Letters from a Hospital Bed

By Jim & Chris Houston

REGENT COLLEGE PUBLISHING
Vancouver, British Columbia

Letters from a Hospital Bed

Regent College Publishing
5800 University Boulevard
Vancouver, BC V6T 2E4 Canada

Regent College Publishing is an imprint of the Regent Bookstore (RegentBookstore.com). Views expressed in works published by Regent College Publishing are those of the author and do not necessarily represent the official position of Regent College (Regent-College.edu).

ISBN: 9781573836050

Inside front cover: Portrait by Sandra Leung, Yaletown Photography.
Inside rear cover: Psalm 1 by Timothy R. Botts®.

Contents

Dedication

This book of letters is dedicated, by Chris, Lydele, Claire, and Penny to the lives and ministries of our parents, Jim and Rita Houston. The ideas and ponderings gathered over Dad's one-hundredth year, each week, by Chris, through emails and conversation with our Dad, were then carefully articulated by Chris. Those of you who knew our Mum will recognize her 'chiming in', from time to time, to ground and add memorable colour to the themes and passions of Dad, that marked his life as father, friend and scholar. We, his children, also have a voice here to articulate the lived faith, love and laughter that was evident in our home. We give this book of personal letters as a gift; they are written to you and for you, to those who knew Mum and Dad, were served by them and whom they welcomed into their home and hearts throughout their long and well-lived lives. To your encounters with them we were often eyewitnesses, even 'eavesdroppers', and so you all, dear readers, have blessed our lives and for each we are grateful.

> Every week, through the writing of these letters, I sought to listen to the soul of my father. Always, the drumbeat of his life and his deep desire to be faithful to his Lord resounded through his often-jumbled thoughts, ringing with a clarity that I have heard for my entire life. My task, as his son, was simply to give him voice and each week speak his heart through crafting these letters. To do so was to discover, as my sister Penny showed me, that I had received and so could now pass on a father's blessing.
>
> Chris Houston, Guelph, December 2023

> My greatest joy with these letters was as I regularly walked in to see my dear Dad, at 99 years old, sitting upright and working diligently at his computer with his bible open and surrounded by his most recent beloved books! With a big smile on his face he would greet me with his latest musings for Chris to share with his readers. He was so happy; his ideas and his stories gave him life. I loved being able to share first hand in his delight. He knows and loves you his readers. It truly amazes me how invested he is in so many of your lives. He wanted to write to you, for you, and I marvelled as the responses

came in at how much connection he had with so many. It was a very special year. I will always be grateful to have been a witness.

Lydele Taylor, Vancouver, December 2023

These letters reflect the heart of Dad as I have seen him throughout my life. They traverse the diversity of his thinking, his curiosity, his passion for seeing the individual in relationship, but most they reflect his devotion to his Lord. Chris has beautifully and creatively given words that speak my Dad's heart. Yet this is only a part of the value of these letters. I have long shared Dad's love of spiritual formation and the early Spiritual Fathers. As a student with teacher, I have been hungry to learn from and to imitate Dad. Letter by letter, week by week, my relationship with Dad grew to partnership – because you wrote back! For as we worked together to respond to the many emails he received, I watched first-hand his heart at work. Through these letters, I have been blessed to interact with so many of friends around the world and now even privileged to call some of you, my friends, too.

Claire Taylor, Midhurst, December 2023

As the youngest, Dad's voice has not always been accessible to me. His language, his vast understanding of and fascination with history, along with my own personal struggle to "hear" my Dad, have meant that I have often missed or simply tuned out what he has spoken. These weekly letters were a wonderful reminder to me of the richness that I have reaped from being a "Houston kid", and Chris' more approachable language has helped me to understand my Dad and his lofty ideas that much better. I am so grateful to my parents for the inheritance of thought and love and to my brother for his "translation" and reminder that yes, I do not only understand, but I embrace our parents' faith, love and passion.

Penny Crosby, Vancouver, December 2023

Preface

> *"You yourselves are our letter, written on our hearts, known and read by everybody. You show that you are a letter from Christ, the result of our ministry, written not with ink but with the Spirit of the living God, not on tablets of stone but on tablets of human hearts."* (2 Cor. 3:2-3, NIV)

In the spring of 1996, during a particularly difficult season in my life, I sat down at a desk in the senior common room of my college in Oxford and wrote a letter to Jim Houston. I well remember the letter I received by return. Jim lovingly redirected me to see my situation differently: God was offering me a different post-doctoral education than I had planned for myself.

I know that many of you have letters like this too from Jim—letters that spoke to you in a deeply personal way at a significant time in your life. Or perhaps it was a conversation you remember. The line rightly blurs between the two, since the personal letter is really just conversation in another mode.

Letters from a Hospital Bed. What could be a more perfect genre for Jim Houston, who has spent a lifetime seeking to emphasize the personal over against the professional? Before anyone was using the word "postmodernism," Jim was aware that the rising generation needed to see the Christian mind as part of the response of the whole Christian person to God and his grace. His whole career was founded on this basic Christian personalism.

No wonder this passed over into a lifetime of intimate conversations and letter-writing. Jim always looked for ways to sustain meaningful, deeply personal interactions with those he met.

It is probably no accident that much of the New Testament is itself made up of letters, and that St. Paul naturally turned to the personal letter as a metaphor for the Corinthian church and their relationship to Christ and to the apostle. A personal letter doesn't pretend to the objectivity of the essay, where the author disappears, or the subjectivity of the diary, where the reader disappears. It is a distinctively *personal* form of communication.

And yet *personal* does not mean insubstantial. A letter really should say something. It is not like a text message: *sup cu l8r k?* (*What's up? See you later, okay?*) It is hard to say whether the digital revolution has introduced a new renaissance in personal communication or has led to new levels of banality—or both.

Certainly, Jim Houston's letter to me in 1996 was both personal and carried a substantial message—even, I dare say, a message that was crafted with, and demanded, careful intellectual reflection. He became a master of the art of letter writing as a form of spiritual direction. And his two-volume *Letters of Faith Through the Seasons: A Treasury of Great Christians' Correspondence* shows just how deeply he was influenced by the form and content of personal letters.

Coming full circle, confined to his hospital room again at the end of his life, with a strong sense that his life was ending as he entered his ninety-ninth year, he looked for a way to send out his messages of encouragement to all of us. Lovingly written, and sometimes creatively crafted from Jim's thoughts by his son Chris, *Letters from a Hospital Bed* is a kind of overheard conversation. It stands as a fitting testament to Jim's life and ministry, and to his heart of love for each one of us. Indeed, these letters may well stir your own memories and help you to recall a significant conversation with Jim.

We in turn have our role to play now, as we pass on what we have received. Jim would want to remind us that each one of us is finally meant to be a letter from Christ himself, written not with pen and ink (or their digital equivalent) by with the Spirit of the living God. *On human hearts . . . from Christ . . . by the Spirit of the living God.* The source of any substantial and personal communication about God is finally the Holy Trinity. And such very personal theology ought in turn to be a blessing to the world, "known and read by everybody," as Paul says.

It is one of the greatest honors of my life to hold the James M. Houston Chair of Spiritual Theology at Regent College, but it has been a much greater honour that Jim considered me his friend in Christ. Jim's legacy of spiritual friendship and conversation lives on in these letters and in the lives of each one of us.

Bruce Hindmarsh
James M. Houston Professor of Spiritual Theology
Regent College

Acknowledgment

To those who wrote in response as these letters were published on-line in 2021/22, thank you! Your encouragement of this content sustained Dad and I through the year of writing together. Your responses so often reflected our shared hearts' desire.

As children of Dad and Mum, especially in these latter years of their lives, we have each played different roles and I am deeply grateful for the loving support of my sisters, Lydele, Claire (who tirelessly managed all the e-mails and postings!) and Penny, as I made my contribution as a writing partner for our father.

Kathy Gillin helped greatly with editing and without the persistent encouragement of Bill Reimer and now, his able successor, Kim Boldt, along with his team at Regent College Publishing, this book would not have been published. Thank-you!

Each week as I wrote, Mum (Rita) chimed in somehow or another with her wise grounding counsel. While she has been gone a few years now, she remains an ever-present practical voice in my head, from whom I also first learned my love for language. Anytime there were too many words, she and I were just playing together!

Yet, above all, I bear witness to the tireless and covenanted support and love of my life-partner, Jeannie. Not only could I not have done this work without her, but I would not be whom I have become.

Chris Houston
Guelph, January, 2024

Editor's Note: An Introduction from your scribe, originally written as an epilogue. It appears there as well, in slightly different form.

Dear friends,

In 2021, my dad and our family set out to explore his 99th year. We began this journey in a very different place than we found ourselves at year's end. Dad had fallen in mid-2021, been hospitalized, and lost his mobility. In retrospect, he was probably not eating properly. He slept a great deal during the day. His spirits were low, and he was quite certain that he just wanted to move to the "hospice" so he could follow Mum home just as soon as the Lord could arrange it, preferably sooner. We wonder sometimes if he expected a chariot to appear like Elijah –"bring me my chariot of fire!"—but the Lord had other plans. Gradually, Dad began to want to read and to write again. My sister Claire and I needed to find a genre that would work for him without requiring the rigors of academic publication.

Letters From a Hospital Bed began as a simple way to enable Dad to once again communicate what was on his heart. His early notes were cryptic and mainly indecipherable, yet they contained gems that I recognized from decades of simply listening to what he thought. I recognized familiar patterns and themes, and they bore a new and urgent edge of growth. His more-than-occasional flights of fancy triggered another awareness as I prepared each letter to send to Claire, who managed all the on-line engagement: The voice of our Mum occasionally chimed in, when earth seemed to have lost any grip and Dad needed to be "grounded" once again. I invented "Editor's notes" to provide a way for Mum to speak her piece from time to time, and occasionally burst a rather "heavenly minded" bubble that needed to be more "earthly good." Some weeks, Dad would send lots of notes. Others, he grew quiet and even silent. Gradually he wrote more, and most blessedly, he began to make more sense again, which helped the editing process considerably. His reading has become once again more voracious, and his once-dispersed library is once again growing, rapidly, mainly with the books of very long-dead people!

And as this letter project accumulated a mailing list of well over 1000 friends around the world, and I re-crafted his notes into the letter genre we had created together, something else happened in me. For many decades, Dad had been a feature in the lives of students and friends that still number in the thousands. This had a consequence for his children: He was much less in our lives than in yours. It was not always easy sharing him with our regular household visitors, let alone with those who arrived through virtual means. Sometimes, as young adults, it was a real relief when he was busy with his teaching and lectures, but that independence wore thin after a while. When we listened to the enthusiasm of others for Dad's favour, we wondered if we might occasionally share it ourselves. For me as his son, this project has been redemptive in so many ways. I want to bear witness to that relationship, to encourage other parents and children to stay faithful to one another through what might be hard years. Sometimes the harvest of patience is long in coming, even taking nearly 70 years in the ripening.

We have all said of Dad's 100th year that in it he grew steadily younger. As 100 neared, he delighted in his renewed mobility and his daily opportunity to tend to the needs of his caregivers. We saw a lovely reciprocity at work, inviting each of us to consider how we might extend grace, in abundance, even from the growing limits of our own age and stage. To this day, Dad yearns to "stay faithful 'til the end." As your scribe, I have sought to be relentless in pursuit of "praxis" to Dad's "thesis," to demand that he encounter for himself the truths that he has wished to convey. Sometimes, I think I quite mystified him with my insistence on needing to "live" his "theology" and to connect what he might be gleaning from a long-dead "patristic," some truth that might help us all deal with culture wars, or the war in Ukraine, or climate change, or the pandemic, or the myriad of harshening realities in a world busy abandoning God. Perhaps my insistence was purely selfish—I needed to know why something mattered, not just that it was interesting—but I hoped that I was representing you all faithfully in my asking. At one point he said, "You are asking me to write autobiographically. It is not what I do!" Perhaps I was, and to his considerable credit, after 99 years he bent to this new task and learned still more. To have shaped my father, even as he has shaped me, brought the project full circle.

With thanks to you all for your patient reading and to my sister Claire, who made all the writing visible. You will find his birthday greeting to you all in our final posting in this series.

Your faithful scribe,

Chris Houston

Section:

I

"In the Pit"

Letters Written from ...
October 2021 – February, 2022

Psalm #1 of Jim (October 2021-February 2022)

1) Lord, I am so very, very tired. May I just come home?

2) When I rose in my bed in the night and fell and was stuck, I felt so frighteningly alone.

No one knocked on my door. No one came by. All the independence that I have for so long prized was of no help as I lay trapped by the side of my bed, unable to cry for help, unable even to know if I would make it through the long day.

3) But then You met me in my dreams. Or, was I awake? It doesn't matter, for You were there, drawing me through Your own suffering, yielding just a tiny taste of Your time upon the cross, opening a crack in the doorway to see from Your timeless place. We were together.

4) You filled my dreams with Your remarkable knowing of me: of wee Jimmie, of James, of Dr. James, of Jim. You knew me all. In this place of helplessness, we grew so much closer, You and I.

5) As the veil thinned, Rita grew closer. I could almost reach out and touch her, hear her voice. Mighty God of tender moments, thank you!

6) And then, my loving children bore me to the hospital where I would soon follow Rita's path heavenward. I could hardly wait! I was so very done.

7) Kind souls encouraged me to eat—but why? Kind souls tended my needs—but why? My kindly gymnast tenderly encouraged my body to move—but why?

8) Long as I might to go home, I lived. I breathed, ate, moved, even laughed.

9) The days of waiting for eternity turned to weeks of living, more living, more eating, more sleeping, more moving … more loving. Eternity on hold, delayed, deferred…at least for now.

10) And a deluge, a tsunami of visitors, turned my hospital room into the reluctant chaos of friendship. (Why are they all here, Lord? Perhaps to say "goodbye"? Do they not know that I have nothing left? Do they not see that I am fading fast? Well, I'd like to be fading …but it just does not seem to be working out that way.)

11) I thought I was ready for You, ready to hear my longed-for "well done," ready to know I had not been "unfaithful to the heavenly vision." It seems that I was wrong. Lord, are You sure? Are You really, really, sure that You want me to stay, that You want me to live, when I was quite sure that I wanted otherwise?

12) It is morning and night now, day after day. Still I breathe in Your grace, and still I see You only through a glass, darkly. And as each day passes, something like strength returns. The hoist tracks so kindly placed above my head for mobility lie wasted. I can walk to the washroom…all ten feet! I even look forward to breakfast with my fellow "inmates."

13) Perhaps I'll see another springtime, just one more. I think, Lord, that would be nice, to see another spring, to even see the sun. Not that it has been absent from me, just I from its light, from its Light. Perhaps, just perhaps, I might not be so quite ready to leave as I thought.

14) But please, if I stay, as I stay, can You please help me find something to do?

Letter #1

Thanksgiving (in the US)

November 25, 2021

Dear friends,

In the past few days, Chris and the other family assembled for my wonderful 99th birthday celebration. Those best wishes, including a cartoon from one dear friend, came just in time to inspire my new book, which to my surprise, my son Chris has suggested I should write! When he was younger, I can still hear him saying to me, "Oh Dad, why do you have to write another book?" Now he and Claire are helping me on a new project. *Letters from a Hospital Bed* will be a new genre, just when I thought I had finished all writing. I have been reflecting on this hospital experience and realizing that all of you, as my worldwide community of friends, have dear ones of your own who are themselves in hospital. For many years, I hated the sight of hospitals. I avoided them. They reminded me so painfully of events in my own childhood that were very difficult. I associated them with blood and blood transfusions, and so they nauseated me. And yet, so many of us must enter these places to be present and caring to our own loved ones. These letters, I hope, will give you some insight into the experience of the one who is hospitalized, as I am now. I hope to encourage you through our own experience of becoming so deeply dependent on the care of others for even the most basic of needs. I have had my good days and some not good at all. And yet through it all, I find the Lord so present and instructing me. Perhaps, by sharing the lessons we are still learning, I can the better be of encouragement to each of you.

This is by way of an experiment, and we will all see how it will unfold. I am not embarking on this project alone. I am working with my son Chris and with my daughter Claire. Chris tells me that for a lifetime he has seen this community of my friends, of which you are each a part, as his "competition" for my attention as his father. In the past months, Chris and I have spent time in conversation together such as we have never before enjoyed, and we have each noticed and known the other as never before. This intimacy for us both is new and fresh, and through it, he shares my compassionate desire that each of you would know the deep love of God that is so faintly reflected in our earthly relationships. And so we are embarking on this project together, as a family—for my other children are in their own ways involved—that as a family we might bring you each joy and encouragement and a deeper knowing of God, "all the more as you see the Day approaching" (Heb. 10:25). As the apostle John, in his prologue, profoundly is communicating about the uniqueness of the Son of God, so he is also recognizing each of us as unique. To have that recognition is to set us free as men and women. For, "if the Son sets you free, you will be free indeed!" (John 8:36) These letters, unlike a book to an audience, are being written to you, as each unique persons, so that you each may know greater freedom in your uniqueness in the Son of God.

Affectionately yours,

Jim

Letter #2

Continuing on Thanksgiving (in the US)

November 25, 2021

Dear friends,

Although my 99th birthday was celebrated with great excitement, yet it was with much sobriety that I entered this celebration. Very recently, I heard that my friend Tony—who sat opposite me here at Point Grey Hospital, every morning at 7:30 for breakfast—suddenly died two nights ago, from heart problems. He used to walk up and down in front of his chair, restlessly. I often wondered why. It must have been the heart pains he was suffering. Why then should God take him when he was only 74 and God keep me when I am now 99? I feel rebuked that I used to wish that the Lord had taken me already, but increasingly, I see that He still has a ministry for me here.

In the weeks ahead, I hope I can write to you all, as a community of dear friends. Many of you I have known for decades. I have always written, as you know, but now I must find yet another voice for this season of my life. And so, I begin a new project with you all and we shall see where it takes us.

Chris asked me, "Why keep writing, Dad?" Why should I do it? I think it is to help Christians not to be afraid of death, for indeed, death is a cruel enemy. We each must meet it, first in those we love and eventually, ourselves. At the beginning of the last century, Christians used to teach about the "rapture," leaving children afraid that during the night, God might take their parents up into heaven and leave them to have their breakfast on their own! I recall an amusing story of D.L. Moody, who received as a gift a baggy suit jacket and pair of trousers. One day a kindly parishioner commented that the Lord "was not anticipating His soon coming when you were given that baggy suit!" No longer do we have that kind of teaching. We believe, instead, that God calls us into our eternal home individually and in unique ways. That is why these letters are being written, as Paul exhorted the Thessalonian Christians: "Therefore encourage one another and build each other up, just as in fact you are doing" (1 Thess. 5:11).

At this stage, I see the Day of Christ approaching for me. I am learning not to rush that day, but to see that even from a hospital bed, I want to speak with a voice of encouragement. When I was a young boy, I spent many long days in hospital, wearied by diphtheria, unable to breathe easily on my own, sometimes sitting in an oxygen tent. Even then, the Lord gave me a desire to see others encouraged and so I wrote small notes on verses, attached to long pieces of string, which I fluttered out the window to be caught by passers-by. It is over 90 years since the heart of that small boy, hampered by his health, sought to encourage others. Now, while hampered by the lack of mobility and other health limitations, my deep heart's desire has changed little; perhaps from my debilitation, there should come encouragement for others. Through the gift of the internet, I no longer need pieces of paper and string to reach for strangers. God has given me a quiver full of friends, of names and families whom each of you represent. So, from my bed, once again, I send good news and the hope that is ours in the gospel of our Lord Jesus Christ. I see Him approach all too clearly, but wish each of you to know the hope we have in Christ.

Affectionately yours,

Jim

Letter #3

Editor's Note: Well, you've surprised us with so many responses to Dad's first notes. Thank you all! Rest assured that Dad and I read each and every one. Many commented on "sharing our Dad." That has been a journey for all four of us, as his kids. It is hard to hear others express a value in our father that we might not have ourselves experienced, but the Lord is giving us time that is unmerited favour. Because Dad is now at Point Grey hospital, where Mum spent her last months, he has even befriended one of the nurses who nursed Mum into the presence of her Lord. She and Dad now have a special bond. He went to die. He was done, unable to express himself as he once did. Yet as you see in his emerging narrative, he continues to learn. This, for his kids, has been one of his remarkable qualities: he has always lived on the edge of what he is still discovering. We want to help him share what he is still discovering now, just as he has always done. It was a shock for us to see him resigned to give up, but now he is back—less lucid, but nonetheless zealous for his life mission.

November 30, 2021

Dear friends,

It is now just one week since my birthday. It was both a sobering and joyful time.

I continue to think about my breakfast partner Tony, who died of a heart attack at just 74. In the past, I too was subject to heart attacks. I no longer have them, because the last serious one was about ten years ago, and what was blocked was the major artery that they call the "widow's artery" because its blockage is often deadly. With new heart technology at that time, a balloon was injected that kept my widow's artery permanently opened, to avoid death. It has secured me ever since. It is that medical intervention that enabled my family and me to celebrate 99 years on November 21.

Some months ago, I came to this hospital where dear Rita spent her last months, because they have hospice care. I came here to die, but I realized through Tony's death that I came here to care and comfort those around me, whoever they are. There is no retirement for those who would live a beatific life; that is, a life that fulfils the beatitudes.

And so as I enter into this 100th year, I hope that even when I am eventually dying, I can still live as a witness to living a beatific life.

I have been haunted by this hope ever since 1964, when I returned from a challenging conference with some students. After my return, God appeared as in an intense light at the foot of my bed. I had the same amazed reaction as Saul of Tarsus, who later cried out "So then, King Agrippa, I was not disobedient to the vision from heaven" (Acts 26:19). It called me to emigrate from Oxford with my family, and though I have had some hard moments emotionally, this text still challenges me to go on living faithfully until I die. It was much more than an academic calling, or a calling according to what I would like to do. It simply binds my life. Since 1964, until when I will be called home eternally, I am like the Old Testament slave whose ear was bored to be always listening and responding—for me, to my Heavenly Father. I am always the eternal servant of God. So, my prayer for each of you is that you have eyes to see and ears to hear that your life is called to serve others because you are the slave of Jesus Christ. Your calling will always be far, far more than a professional interest. You will find yourself united beyond all professional interest, united within yourself and with your Lord. You will not be what Scripture describes as "double-minded and unstable in all they do" (James 1:8). This is the reality that the mystics like Theresa of Avila experienced. She stepped forward in her meditations from being "in love with Christ" to being "married to Christ." It is an eternal union.

As I recognize the enormous gift and privilege of a gift of long life, I wish you each every blessing of Christ.

Affectionately yours,

Jim

Letter #4

Editor's Note: It was with some bemusement that I found Dad on a recent morning up, dressed, sitting alert in his chair, waiting for me to arrive. "Get the machine" (his laptop), he said. "I have a story." I jumped to it, opened his laptop and sat awaiting his narrative. It is not every morning, with only one flat white coffee between deep sleep and sitting alert with a keyboard, that I find myself immediately around a Neolithic campfire in southern Italy, complete with bean vines growing over stone walls, newly fired clay pots to boil a primitive soup, interspersed with memories of camping holidays that I was supposed to remember from the age of 4 or 5. All this inspired by Dad's recent consumption of his lunch the day before. I tried hard to draw a line connecting the "trullo" (look it up; I had to!), Neolithic man, bean soup, and deep spiritual enlightenment for his friends around the world. Dad was certain this had great significance for us. It did for him, at any rate. I confess I found the thread just a tad hard to follow, but I have learned not to question the mysterious ways of God, including the occasionally unfathomable labyrinth of our father's mind. Perhaps, white bean soup (either modern or ancient) will connect for you in ways that his more Philistine kids might have missed. We seek to be faithful in retelling, if not always successful in interpretation!

December 1, 2021

My dear friends,

Just recently, while enjoying white bean soup for my lunch, I was reminded of taking my young family to the south of Italy. This region is remarkably stony with little soil, and the local diet often includes a white bean soup. Where grown locally, the bean plants trail over the low stone walls of the stone houses—referred to as "trullo." As a young family, we enjoyed a few days spent living in a "trullo" where, in the hot climate, the house is cool by day and by night. As a geographer, I had read about the origin of this particular white bean soup at the Centre for the Study of Domesticated Plants, in Paris. This soup is one of the oldest recipes of its kind in the world and had been the result, in Neolithic times, of the first use of fire in this ancient region, which enabled Neolithic man to first shape bowls from clay and then boil this particular soup. As I recounted this memory to my nurse while eating my lunch, she wondered whether I was simply making this up. No, I replied, its all quite true. "Oh my goodness," she said, "I can no longer call you just 'Jim,' I must call you 'professor.'" I protested and assured her that she must continue to call me Jim, for I am still a human being, just as she is. Perhaps, next time you are wandering the grocery aisles in search of something that might rescue you from the trivialities of mere post-modernity, you might reach for the white bean soup and join the entire panoply of Western Civilization in the celebration of this ancient meal!

On a recent morning, I was listening to my son and realizing that we can be very privileged to be bound in bed, having all the time in the world, to listen to one's children express their intimate experiences of the Lord, in contrast to when you are running about, all very busy but with no time to really hear them. The story that Christopher was telling me was a unique story about himself, a rare experience of knowing God's joy in him. The story is too private to share, but we had, also from the hospital bed, a very moving experience together: Lying on the horizontal, I could look straight into his eyes and hear him say, "I have seen you see me, notice me, not writing and reading as always, but because you are in bed, you are noticing me." These are precious moments in my day. I wonder how you each might find the space to look your loved ones in the eye and know them and be known by them.

Affectionately yours,

Jim

Letter #5

December 3, 2021

Dear friends,

One of the advantages of being "on the horizontal" in bed is that you share intimate stories as you look at each other in the eye, with a reciprocity that we do not often experience. It is like the experience of the psalmist: "But I have calmed and quieted myself, I am like a weaned child with its mother" (Ps. 131:2). When I was at the major local public hospital during a recent stay of three weeks, I was looked after by more than a dozen different nurses of diverse ethnic backgrounds. As I watched them, I saw how they struggled with their diversity. Their cultural backgrounds shaped how they cared for the patients. The difficulties they had with each other was that they had such contrasting modes of caring, reflecting different temperaments and emotions. They were not understanding each other.

Here, in this small private hospital where I now stay, there is much less diversity among the different backgrounds and a much more consistent caring model, based largely on their Filipino heritage. I am finding that I am getting to know them, almost as if I were one of their relatives. Ironically, I can be more intimate with them than I can be with my own family. In a family, we take each other for granted, but these nurses know me more intimately because of the kinds of care that they give to me. I have no regrets of being with them in this caring place, because I am learning that it is through this very personal caring that real intimacy grows. With my family, as I enter into this deeper vulnerability of my personal needs, I also find a growing intimacy as they witness my deeper physical dependence.

When Jesus took up the towel and washed the disciples' feet, he showed us that it is in the very personal acts of caring for one another that real intimacy grows. Yes, partnership and collaboration are borne of work together, but to truly know and to be truly known, we must enter into a much deeper and much more personal caring for one another's basic needs. At this stage of my life, my physical limitations offer me little choice, but I see its fruit as I discover deeper layers of intimacy with those who in many ways are strangers and yet are far from strangers; they are fast becoming my dearest friends. As you reflect on your own communities, on the various estrangements that we all experience (and that I know have burdened many of you for so long), I urge you to take the risk of being attentive to the other in very simple and basic ways of caring. "A cup of cold water" is often more than enough if we but pause and take the risk of making the offer.

Sending you all much love,

Jim

Letter # 6

December 16, 2021

Dear friends,

In so many ways, our everyday language gives us clues into some of the deep-seated assumptions that so often unconsciously guide our attitudes and actions. I have been reflecting on this in a simple phrase with which I became familiar as an adult, "Happy Xmas." Once, we had a sense of freedom to express "Happy Christmas." Then we dropped the Christ and substituted an "X." Now, we have dropped the term completely and greet each other with "Happy Holidays." To be sure, we are but reflecting the rapid secularization of our culture; but as Christians, we risk losing our own identity in this loss of sheer wonder at the enormous mystery that is the Incarnation. I suspect that beneath our simple language changes there lies a seeping loss of confidence in our own faith, at a time when confidence in faith is more deeply needed than at any time before.

This pandemic—which has swept aside some of our most cherished habits and practices and has disrupted commerce, food supplies and all manner of other essentials—has also been a remarkable instrument of the grace of God. I am reminded of the observations of the Earthkeeping Institute: that industrial emissions were so reduced by shutdowns earlier in the year, that we saw the creation already begin to recover. Each of you, in so many ways, has seen new life emerge out of the suffering in this time of global travail. Somehow, we have all both lost and gained so much that has surprised us; and this disorientation, even this discontent, prepares us to welcome the Christ of Advent who comes to us not in triumph but so handicapped, so vulnerable that He was unable to even feed and clothe Himself. I think I understand this vulnerability better now than ever I did before.

Where I live, everyone is old. Some are very old. Their bodies may not be up to much, but they still have a remarkable capacity to complain! "It is no fun being old." "It is no fun being deaf." I can join in this lament. I know I am old and deaf and can no longer enter into the chatter of my grandchildren and their children. When my masked visitors appear, I can hardly hear or understand what they say. I have been reflecting on what our gospel physician, Luke, may teach me about such grumbling. He also teaches me about holiness: not mine, but that of Christ—Lord of all—the one laid so low as to be without any capacity to care for himself. Utterly dependent. Only He is holy, and so my grumbles and complaints fade into inconsequence of my own sinfulness before Messiah. I am reminded of the younger sister of Corrie ten Boom, in prison, ready to be killed by the Nazis, complaining to Corrie about the fleas in their mattress, to which her older sister replied, "Thank God for the fleas, which is why the guards leave us alone so that our other sisters can join us for Bible study and prayers together."[1]

Some years ago, when Chris and I were teaching in Brazil, I was asked by one of the conference participants as to what I attributed my long life. Chris reminds me today that I gave only a one-word answer: "Gratitude." There is a simple chorus that I love that reminds us:

Count your blessings,
Name them one by one,
And it will surprise you
What the Lord has done.[2]

May I encourage us all, even in the midst of this confusing season of loss and gain, with too much that is so unfamiliar, to see in this mysterious Incarnation that we celebrate, a call for overflowing gratitude. That is the cry of my heart. There is so much that I can no longer do, but with all I have I will still boldly declare, "Merry Christ-mas" to you all!

Most hopefully yours,

Jim

Letter # 7

Editor's Note: The genesis of this letter was an email soon followed by two phone calls from Dad, asking me to provide him with the website address for Wikipedia. Then he called back again, forgetting that I had provided him with what he needed, to tell me, again twice, that he did not need me to worry about getting him the website. He had found it on his own. In the end, he wrote just 35 words from his urgent research. What had caught Dad's attention was the western custom of making new year's resolutions. Coming so close on the heels of the all-too-secularized Incarnation celebration of Christmas, Dad was bothered that we were all losing the plot and he wanted to refresh his own memory as to the origins of the New Year's custom of resolutions. While his capacity for rigorous research has largely faded to a quick reference to Wikipedia, his passion that we should at all times and in all circumstances think "Christianly"—as he once would have put it—is as vibrant and vigorous as ever. This letter reflects his urgent sense that we must enter the newness of this next year not with the resolutions of our own capacity but with a deepening dependence on the Lord, the giver of all Life.

December 28, 2022

Dear friends,

As a child, I have vivid memories of Christmas; yet I have always wondered why it was that I was taught so much about Christmas and so little about New Years. I had heard from an early age that the celebration of the new year involved the making of promises that I would be good, and yet I have no recollection of anyone being able to explain why such promises should be made. Nevertheless, and as a good Scot who knew to celebrate Hogmanay, I always had a sense that the event was important but I had never bothered to explore this question… until now!

It might strike you as odd that at 99 this should be the subject of my curiosity. My son Chris has a sign up in his office in his home that says, "The cure for boredom is curiosity. There is no cure for curiosity." I suppose that, were I not curious, I should be bored and so, instead, I am curious, in this instance, about a festival that has been celebrated around me for nearly a century while I never once stopped to wonder about its origins. So, thanks for the Wikipedia contributors who help us all!

There, online, I learned that the origins of the "new year's resolutions" are Roman at least, perhaps earlier. It became customary to make promises to the gods to repay debts and return borrowed objects. The Romans made promises to their god Janus, from whom we find the month January named. Later in medieval times, the knights reaffirmed their commitment to chivalry in the "peacock vow." Still today, many of us make such resolutions. Sadly, most do not keep them. It all seems like rather a frivolous waste of time, and I can now well understand why it remained a mystery for so long. And so I have been wondering: What do I do as I enter this new year that marks this moment in my life?

We live today in a culture of rampant individualism and fierce personal independence. Our personal capacity to choose independence is celebrated, fought over, and hyped in ads and in political speeches. Everywhere, I am encouraged to be my own god. Yet, as I lie here in my hospital bed, dependent on others to serve many of the needs of my own body that I used to address for myself, there is something quite absurd, quite laughable about all this celebrated individualism. As if, now that there is so little that I can choose alone, I am somehow dead, of less value, even less "human." Far from it! I am reminded of a trip that I took with dear Rita early in our lives together, when we visited Mars Hill in Athens. I can hear her voice reading from 1 Corinthians 15, Paul's confident declaration of the historical resurrection of Christ. And the text in the Acts of Apostles where Paul speaks, "People of Athens…you are ignorant of the very thing you worship—and this is what I am going to proclaim to you" (Acts 17:22-23). We have no need to make promises we cannot keep when the Lord has made a covenant with us that "gives us the victory through our Lord Jesus Christ…Let nothing move you … give yourselves fully to the work of the Lord" (1 Cor. 15:57-58).

In many respects, December 31 is in no way particularly different from January 1, especially here in the seniors' hospital home where I live. The daily routine will and must continue and yet, 2022 may well mark the year that I return to an eternal presence with the God who made me unique, who knew of my days when there were none, and who knows the time and moment when my time will be complete. Many others know the marked time of cancer or other disease that inexorably consumes the available days, and while we soon will mark a new year, it will be as unknown as the many before. And so, I find myself marking the new year not with grand promises—most of which are never kept—but with a resolved stillness and a patience to wait expectantly for Christ to come.

I am reminded of the exhortations of Gregory of Nazianzus who, in his 38th Oration, encourages us "not to adorn our doors with garlands, or lead dances nor decorate our streets…but to feed on the delicacies of the law of God, and with those discourses which are particularly appropriate for this present festival."[3] May we pray that the festivities of this week not crowd out the true celebration of the Christ Child, singing with George Herbert the 17th-century poet, "Iesu is in my heart, his sacred name is deeply carved there."[4]

In earlier months of this year now ending, I have been far more eager to die than I find myself now. It not that I am no longer weary with the work of this life, but as long as the Lord gives me breath, I want to use it to be urgent for His glory. Isaiah 55:6 reminds me to "seek the Lord while he may be found" and so as we enter a new year, I urge each of us not to make false promises to long-dead gods but to seek Him who knows us each so well and holds our identity safely in His hands.

Go well, dear friends, into this good new year, not because you have resolved much but because your Heavenly Father, through Christ, has redeemed much.

With my blessings,

Jim

Editor's Note: Dad is just loving your letters to him. They have invigorated his life in many of the ways in which you have described that he infused your own. This is a very reciprocal mercy! God has built a very circular "economy" in your lives as his friends.

Letter #8

Editor's note: The theme of this letter Dad has identified as his "next book" albeit, as he observes, "a short one." We find that Dad's "books" are getting shorter and shorter, yet stripped of much of their academic embellishment, they better reveal the essence of the message—more simply and, perhaps, more accessibly for those of us who might have struggled to find the plot in more esoteric tomes. As we explored the origins of this theme today, we wish you could sense the energy behind his exhortation to "wait upon the Lord and renew your strength, you shall mount up with wings, like eagles." We saw it in his eyes, heard it in his voice, all of him unconsciously desirous that more could be done to give glory to the divine revelation of God and so we say, with him, "Thine be the Glory!"

January 6, 2022

My dear friends,

Recently, as I lay dozing in the evening, I found myself praying and asking the Lord "what is my next book?" As a geographer, I have always been exploring things, both physical and spiritual. The Lord made me inquisitive. It is simply who I am and so, what I do. So, I was waiting, dozing, praying, anticipating the promise of the prophet Isaiah, that those who wait upon the Lord, shall renew their strength, they shall mount up with wings, like eagles. I have learned to live day by day, awaiting the manna that comes from heaven on which I have learned to feed daily. And so it came to me, that which I find myself now curious...what lies behind the Genesis stories, the characters that we know so well, and the settings of Cain and Abel, Abraham and Isaac and Jacob? The need struck me and fired my imagination, because I could not recall any commentaries that explored this theme.

I have been wondering about the characters of Cain and Abel. Cain, the one of the land, comes to symbolize independence from God. The brilliant engineering of Egyptian irrigation systems represents a substitute for deep dependence on the rain that must nurture the shepherd's pasture. Abel, the shepherd, knows no such independence—and so our Lord leads His people out from the land of irrigation, a land of independence from God, to the land of pastures, of dependence and of the voice of the shepherd. Here in these ancient stories, we find the origins of our sin, in the substitution of our own genius for a deepening dependence upon our Father who sustains all. As I explore this question, I am seeking to better understand one of the young Pharaohs whom, as I recall, was a believer in one god and not the animal pantheon of Egyptian deities. His reign was short, and he likely was poisoned for his doctrinal deviance. Perhaps God came to him in a dream, even as he came to me in my recent reverie. I'm now seeking to learn more about him so that we might better grasp the significance of these iconic characters to our faith.

This shepherd archetype, to which I aspire as I wait for the daily nourishment that sustains my soul, runs all through the scriptures. It is the archetype of dependence, of waiting, of not trusting in our own sufficiency to supply our needs. Despite all our own proficiency and cultivated expertise, we are invited not to rest on what we can accomplish but to wait for the manna and the rain that sustain. As I am finding, even when stripped of much of that with which I was once more capable, the Lord meets us daily as we wait for Him to feed us, and I can once again mount up with wings, like eagles. I can run and not be faint. My prayer for each of you is that you too may know such dependence and zeal for living.

Affectionately yours,

Jim

Letter #9

January 13, 2022

Dear friends,

I have been increasingly sensing the need to pay attention to the simple rhythm of the calendar and to ask, "What day is this, and how then might I live in the company of others who have gone before?" My own book, Letters of Faith through the Seasons, has been a helpful guide. Last Thursday, January 6, was the first day of the Epiphany season. That led me to ask, "What does this day mean for me today?"

Our word "Epiphany" derives from the Greek word *epiphaiea,* which I interpret as "manifestation." Just as Christmas is the season of God becoming human, so Epiphany is the manifestation of God, the very human Christ, starting to have an impact. His human presence in our world stirred three astrologists, deemed wise in their culture (and so "magi"), to go and seek where He was located. What made them wise was that they sought a "reality" beyond the assumed knowledge of their contemporaries. They were wise because they recognized what they did not know, what they did not comprehend. Their hunger drove them to seek for something beyond themselves. The heart of their wisdom was a mobilizing awareness of their ignorance, and they left all to seek what they knew was there to be found but which they had not yet discovered. They saw, but they had not yet fully seen.

One year on this day of Epiphany, in a small village church with Norman origins, a community gathered to lay to rest my niece, Sheila. As with the Magi, most of the world did not notice. Sheila was born with her umbilical cord around her neck, which briefly but critically starved her of oxygen and so harmed her new-born brain. As a result, there was much that she could not do. The injury set her apart and required much specialized care throughout her 63 years of life. Yet Sheila was wise, for she lived like a philosopher, seeing things that others did not see. She saw, with joy, the lovely image of God that had been planted in all whom she met, and so she loved much. She saw, with wonder, all that her Heavenly Father had made in creation, even in the "postage stamp" of her garden, and so she rejoiced much. She saw, with delight, the vast reservoirs of Jesus's love for her, and so she worshipped much. Sheila was also one of the Magi.

As I now find myself in bed, "on the horizontal" more than ever before, I am perhaps beginning to see as Sheila saw. It is this horizontal plane that opens my eyes, not the vertical. In being more still, more unable, I see more...and I want to be wiser. Like Job, I am also surrounded by the influences that are represented by Job's friends in that ancient text. When Job finds himself stripped of all his material "wealth," his friends ask, "Why would a good God do bad things to good people?" Surely, where there is effect, there must be cause—as any good historian would tell us. Eliphaz searches for faults. Bildad searches for secrets. Zophar searches for the legitimacy to argue with God and demands of Job, "Would [a wise person] argue with useless words" (Job 15:3)?

No-one answers his question for over a thousand years, until, atop Mars Hill in Athens, the apostle Paul, defending himself against the might of the Greek philosophers, answered for us all. "What no eye has seen," he answers Bildad, "what no ear has heard," he answers Zophar, "and what no human mind has conceived," he challenges Eliphaz, "the things God has prepared for those who love Him" (1 Cor. 2:9). Against all the false standards of wisdom and revered competence, the Magi sought what they alone knew they had not yet seen. Against all the false standards of success, my niece Sheila gloriously entered the presence of her Lord with immense and profound confidence. From this place of seeming diminishment through age and physical limitation, I now see from the horizontal what I could not see so clearly when more active. May we too, each in our own ways of hunger, seek for Him who can be found, and so join the Magi.

This is what we celebrate with this season of Epiphany!

Affectionately yours,

Jim

Letter #10

January 20, 2022

Dear friends,

As in so many other places, we have been back in "lock down" again with the Omicron variant. Here where I live, visitors have been severely restricted. Even my own children have been unable to visit, so I have been spending even more time alone. These kinds of times challenge my sense of "proximity" and what it means for me to be with someone, even when they are not physically present. When my wife Rita died and I was no longer able to be with her, in one sense, I realized that she was now in the presence of the Lord. Now, when I am "alone," I too sense the Lord's close presence. In a whole new way, Rita and I are more together. The closer I stay with the Lord, the closer Rita seems to me, for the Lord's presence binds us both closer to Him and I so I miss her less. Time and again, restraint and a sense of loss open up new vistas of discovery.

As I am less able to pursue the things I once did as a professional adult, I hear Christ's invocation, more imperative, that I become like a little child. In John 3, Jesus insists to Nicodemus, "You must be born again," not once, but again and again, in every season, in every day. Nowadays, we tend to think that to be a "serious Christian," we need to hear serious theologians preach every Sunday morning or attend serious teaching on the Apostles of the New Testament, or by exegeting the four Gospels. But the early Church, in educating their own children in home churches, as Jerome, Basil and other early Fathers attest, saw Jesus at the various stages of His own life, first as a child, then later as a mature man, teaching them. Indeed, Jesus had to teach His own earthly Mother *who he was,* while she wonderfully nurtured and fed Him. In the upside-down Kingdom of God, little children often do the teaching.

Aelred of Rievaulx (1110-1167), a pupil of Bernard of Clairvaux, reflects on the child Jesus—and how, when his parents were on their way to Jerusalem to celebrate the Passover, they lost sight of their young son. I am brought to the theme of Matthew 18: All disciples of Jesus must become as little children. Hans Urs von Balthasar has more recently taught us in his wonderful small book, *Unless You Become Like This Child*. This vital insight, which I and all of us need, is exemplified by Jesus the Child, as well by Him as the Son of God. As Matthew 18:2 reports, "He called a little child to him, and placed the child among them," as a prototype, answering Nicodemus's question, "How shall a man be born again when he is old?" (the answer of which lies in John 3:16). We have to be "born again." It all begins with love—the love of God for the Son, as the love of parents for each other, that then produces the child. This is what it is to become a disciple of Jesus, to be immersed in Love, like a child. I have been reflecting on the traits of this "childhood."

ADORATION. The parents adore their child, while the child reciprocates with adoration. This occurs with every birth, where the newborn's visual focal length is 16 inches, so as to best look into the eyes of a mother, as the eyes of a mother look to her child, in mutual recognition. So Jesus, with childlike amazement, looks up to His Heavenly Father, saying, "the Father is greater than I" (John 14:28)! And so in the Father, Christ can have infinite trust.

GRATITUDE. Parents often, as soon as a child can speak, teach them to say "thank you." So, 1 Thessalonians 5:18 reminds us, "give thanks in all circumstances."

MYSTERY. For who could argue with God's Word? A child has no idea where its food comes from. We can never stop accepting it gratefully.

TIME. As we grow up, we are given time to become who we are. As the book of Ecclesiastes outlines, we can never stop growing as a Christian.

Hampered as we all might be these days in our distracting "adult" pursuits, perhaps God is inviting us to be more childlike. And so, let us join with Charles Wesley and affirm:

> Gentle Jesus, meek and mild,
> Look upon a little child;
> Pity my simplicity,
> Suffer me to come to Thee.[5]

With my blessings on your "child-like" hearts,

Jim

Letter #11

January 27, 2022

Dear friends,

Editor's Note: This week, we thought it was only right and real for us to reflect the current reality for Dad. While he has been working on his writing for Easter, he has been quite challenged in this last phase of lockdown for the Omicron variant because of the lack of visitors. He has some engagement through emails and phone calls, but in the absence of in-person interaction, we notice that he struggles to remain present in a current sense. In the next few weeks, we will share some material that he has been working on for a while. We wondered about starting that this week, but we realize, as his friends, he can be with you as he really is—which is more withdrawn and under-challenged by the routine of his daily life. The other day, he talked about being bored with the routine. I can't remember ever hearing our Dad say he was "bored!" Never in over 60 years! We find that he thrives on the stimulus of questions, of invitations to address a question or an issue. As many of you know who have invited him to write or lecture on a subject, he heads off in all kinds of different directions than you may have intended, but the question is an on-ramp and Dad has been missing his familiar "on-ramps." Like booster rockets, inquiry fuels his engine and then it kicks into high gear, still, to this day. So, for this "letter" we thought we would just share where we are all at and invite your questions, your stimuli to Dad, to enquire his reflections on a subject or an issue. Feel free to post below, or send by email. In this way, we can shape a dialogue around, not from, his hospital bed.

With thanks,

Jim's family

Letter #12

Editor's note: The next few letters will explore the subject of dreams. Dad began this subject with the intention to "write a book," as he has so often, and as motivates him today. The content, while instructive, is simply not something that Dad can handle anymore to the appropriate level of scholarship worthy of more traditional publication. This is proving to be a challenging realization to land for him, after a lifetime of academic work, so we continue to explore ways to encourage his discovery, his reflection on what he is learning, and his transmittal and sharing of that reflection for the edification of his friends. Sometimes, repetition of insights—which might be considered evidence of poor editing in more scholarly texts—is actually the meta-narrative that needs to be conveyed, for such repetition reveals Dad's deeper conviction, like the axis around which an issue turns.

January, 2021

My dear friends,

In recent months, I have been reflecting on the experience of dreams. Rarely have I taken them very seriously, but a recent spiritual encounter has awoken a memory of another deeply significant life experience for me and that, together with some other events, has caused me to ask, "Why should Christians take dreams seriously?" None of the Old Testament prophets could have carried out their ministry of rebuking rebellious Israelite kings and their followers without the inspiration and even instructions of their dreams. Psalm 121:4 reminds us that "he who watches over Israel will neither slumber nor sleep." So why then don't Christians have more teaching, preaching, and writing about dreams? The Incarnation narrative, in the birth of Jesus, upon which we reflect at this time of year, all began with dreams to Mary and Joseph. In the biblical narrative, dreams matter. Perhaps they need to matter more to us as well.

It all started for me earlier in the year, when I replaced my winter blanket on my bed, for the summer. My daughter Claire, while flying the oceans as a flight attendant, kept herself occupied on the layovers by quilting a bed cover. One night, as I was praying for them, I suddenly realized that Claire had sewn squares with the outline of the hands of each of my seven grandchildren. Beside each hand was a prayer, a scripture reference each had chosen on the quilt. I was being covered with their prayers, while I was nightly praying for them! What a new bond of faith, hope, and love this going to sleep became! I began to ask the Lord to shape my dreams, to grant me good dreams.

Wonderfully, nightmares and bad dreams, full of one's ego, seem to have disappeared, dreams that previously had continued to distress a mind that was not "in Christ Jesus." It was as if my sleeping life was now "born again," and that a further deepening of consciousness was needed if I were to have "the mind of Christ." I began to explore how my own Christian identity might be shaped by this deepening unconscious encountering of God.

In late summer, after my bed cover had given me many remembrances of my grandchildren as I went to sleep, I had a much more challenging encounter. I do not really recall what happened in detail, only that I fell while getting out of my bed and somehow wedged my body, jammed by a cramped foot, into the small space at the side of my bed. There I lay, unable to move on my own, for over eight hours before I was found by my daughter Penny. The pain in my foot was so intense that I fell into a place between consciousness and unconsciousness. There God met me. In this dream I saw Christ upon His cross, and beside Him stood an empty cross onto which our Lord invited me to join Him in His suffering. I felt no fear in this invitation, only joy to be with the Lord. I vividly recall accepting His invitation, one I interpreted to imply I was to leave my earthly body. While I sensed the Lord's welcome, I confess to some confusion that I find myself still here, waiting to discover what God holds in store for me until His invitation is fulfilled. The three weeks of hospital rest that followed did little to diminish the deep sense of reverence and awe in this encounter, one matched in my own experience only by the encounter at the Urbana mission conference in the early 1960s. It is as vivid today as then. I was, at that time, in discussions with a secular university that wanted me to work with them in adopting the tutorial method of teaching in which I was immersed in Oxford. I had explained that I would want to share my experience in the context of my Christian faith, a condition that proved to be unacceptable to the university. It was during a night of this career cross-roads that I was woken by a very bright light at the foot of my bed. I felt compelled to respond with a question "Lord, what would you have me to do?" From that moment, I began to see the doors that would lead to the foundation of Regent College begin to open. When we pay attention to God, He reveals Himself to us.

In my next letter, I hope to explore what I have learned from others on the importance of dreaming. In the meanwhile, perhaps this letter might prompt your own reflection of ways in which the Lord has spoken uniquely to you through the twilight of consciousness in sleep.

Affectionately Yours,

Jim

Letter #13

Editor's Note: Dad has been very insistent that this material on dreams be communicated. We struggle to faithfully represent both his wishes and the reality that his sense of the substance of what he has prepared, while in essence material, lacks the intellectual rigor of his previous scholarship. There is a pattern in these many avenues of inquiry that capture Dad still, almost daily. He notices something, is curious, explores to his own satisfaction, applies a Christian mind, forms a sense of urgency for others to grasp what he has himself just discovered, and seeks to express his exhortation in some way. We see this again and again. Once, this could be expressed as what is recognized as "scholarship," yet even without the disciplined research and other practices of the academy, this yearning for the other to learn what he himself is just now discovering continues unabated. It is a life force in Dad, and it sustains him in a remarkable way. While he might not still meet the exacting standards of the classroom and the publishing community, his deep desire to explore, discover, and share remains intense, persistent, and unrelenting. For Dad, to be alive is to daily stretch across the threshold of discovery and to marvel at the boundarylessness of the knowing of God. This is the meta-narrative of these letters, an invitation to us all to never cease from exploring the mind of God, even when our "faculties" might impose limits on our capacities.

February 10, 2022

My dear friends,

In my last letter, I explored some of the personal dimensions of dreams that have had an impact on my own life and still do, to this day. My experience and my boundless curiosity have led me to explore what some others have considered important with respect to dreams.

My reading within the discipline of neuroscience has impressed on me the importance of sleep, that it enriches a diversity of functions, including our ability to learn, to memorize, and to make logical decisions. Then, during our day, we can make wise decisions and have a cool-headed exposure to all social challenges. Yet, much of our population in the western world routinely sleeps less than 6-7 hours, which is reported to impact our immune systems, blood sugar balance and other vital systems. It appears that dreaming may be instrumental in preventing some mental illnesses and inhibiting a tendency to delay the onset of Alzheimers.

In Tibet, the Buddhist mindset—aware of being Buddhist day and night, and that their identity persists through wakefulness and sleep—would critique our Western orientation that tends to discount this vital time of unconsciousness. As Christians, we have more than 700 references in the Scriptures to dreams. The prophets could never have done their ministry without this vital guidance. The incarnation was directly facilitated by the dream of Joseph not to put Mary away. In the Psalms, we are reminded that "he who watches over Israel will neither slumber nor sleep" (Ps. 121:4). Whether we are awake or asleep with our dreams, He is communicating with us as He did with the Biblical prophets whose messages from God came when they were asleep.

My desire is to encourage you to explore this vital area of your life even as I, in my own 100th year, find that I must explore it for my own needs. As our God neither slumbers nor sleeps, so too we Christians should see the amazing benefit offered in the realm of our dreams to enrich our Christian identity. We should be aware of our identity as Christians, night or day. That is why, when we go to sleep, our primary prayer should be, "Lord, may I wake up conscious that I am in your presence 24 hours a day. Amen." I encourage you to pray for dreams, to expect the Lord to speak and to be Lord of your unconsciousness just as He is Lord of your waking. I hope, in my next letter, to share some of the practices that have helped me, and which even today are a vital part of my living before the Lord.

Affectionately Yours,

Jim

Letter #14

Editor's Note: In a recent conversation, Dad related greeting his night-time care givers, whose duties are to attend to their patients' bodily needs, with an invitation to pray for them in their work. So, before they helped Dad in ways upon which he is now dependent, he prayed for them, thanking God for their kindness and grace, blessing their ministry of service. As we spoke together about this, he impressed on me our endless opportunities to be the eyes and words of Christ for all with whom we meet, perhaps especially the kind nurses who attend Dad in the night.

February 17, 2022

My dear friends,

I continue to enjoy and anticipate sensing and appreciating the Lord in the night. So often, our sense of night is one of being alone, of longing for sleep in the midst of unwelcome wakefulness, of waking distressed by what our unconscious mind seems to choose for us, leaving us the residue of disturbance and disquiet. At this stage of my life, I find that I enter into sleep without really knowing whether I will wake or on what side of this "veil" I will find myself next. When my beloved Rita died, many of you asked me whether I mourned over her death. It is true that I missed her physical presence and her acerbic wit, which kept me straight for decades, but I also sensed her presence because the thin membrane that separated us was just that, thin. And so I began to dream more about Rita and to sense a deep closeness with her that shifted my sense of loss at her death. All I needed was deep sleep in order to dream, and I learned that I needed to create space for this important practice.

Since I have come into this new home for what I think of as "hospice care"–inasmuch as I do not expect to ever leave here, in this life—I find that my dreams are lessened by the more frequent night-time interruptions from my caregivers. It is an irony that while their focus is to give me physical care at night, I find I need the silence of deep sleep to allow my dream life to be more active. My communion with God is deeper when I dream, and my sense of identity in Christ is strengthened through no actions of my own, other than to entrust myself to the Father in deep sleep. While asleep, little is required of me, but before sleep, there is much I can do. I have learned not to fill my senses with images and sounds that so imprint themselves on my mind that I am then preoccupied with their processing. Instead, I read the psalms and welcome the descent into sleep. Or perhaps I reflect on a beautiful image, such as that iconic hand painted on the ceiling of the Sistine Chapel that affirms we are "imago Dei"–made in God's image.

Earlier, I wrote of how dreams have changed my life and through this, even events that have shaped others. The early indigenous explorers who discovered New Zealand were responding to "a dreaming." Augustine and his mother Monica found themselves united through having had the same dream that they were both, together, in the presence of the Lord, a reality that Augustine explored more fully in his Confessions. The silence of Quakers often led to shared dreams that had profound social impacts, such as the abandonment of slavery, as they recognized through dreams the universal equality of each person, each made uniquely in the image of God. In a time when we think that Zoom is our only way of being "together," perhaps the Lord has other ways for us to enjoy a communion that our busyness has too long resisted. Martin Luther King energized a generation and more, by declaring so memorably that "I have a dream." In our hyper-cognitive times, in which the rational brain is amplified and cognition celebrated, where is the place of our emotions, even the deep depression expressed by Kierkegaard? In our dreams, our emotional life can find greater freedom of expression.

As I have entered this more sleep-filled season of my life, I sense a greater urgency to attend to my dreaming, not only because there is more opportunity—I sleep a lot more—but because I am discovering a richness of life that I was too busy to engage as fully before. I was always blessed by being raised in Spain, where the "siesta" was a daily feature that I have recovered more fully in later life. But dreams are not only for the old. "Young men will see visions," says the prophet Joel (2:28). I see dreams as a double consciousness that can intensify our identity as Christians, to take our faith beyond the simple affirmation of catechism and entrust our entire unconsciousness into the loving arms of our Heavenly Father. It is hard to argue with God in a dream! Instead, we can know His gentle guidance and prodding of our stubborn wills.

As we prepared this letter, Chris has pressed me to express my deep desire for you with respect to our dreaming. In response to his well-intentioned pestering, I make this my prayer for you.

Dear Father, as my friends that read this letter enter their sleep—as they seek for it, even long for it—may they expect Your presence. May they each invite the Lord to enter their unconsciousness, to impress upon them Your knowing of them, of their uniqueness, and to affirm in them the precious identity that they have in Christ so that, even though their conscious minds might be ever creative in resisting Your Love, their dreams might be the place where they are known most deeply. Amen

Affectionately Yours,

Jim

Letter #15

February 24, 2022

Dear friends,

I well remember when I first moved from living on my own home, to my independent apartment where meals and some support were provided. I was excited to think of new ministry opportunities with new friends who were part of my new neighbourhood. It did not turn out as I originally hoped. There were a few glimmers of common interest, but not many. It frustrated me then. I understand it better now. To be fully alive, when your body is less and less interested or capable, becomes not only challenging, but a source of a deep weariness. I have never really subscribed to the "once and done" sense of the familiar phrase "be born again." Over and over in my life, the Lord has opened new doors, revealed new vistas, allowed me to enter new landscapes of both mind and soul. And so it has been again, more recently, for as less and less was possible, I have seen more and more. So much newness, that on many days I sense being "born (yet) again"!

One of the ways in which my dear wife Rita had a disproportional influence on our family was to train our children to tease me as mercilessly as she, in her own way, did herself. As I started to explore and edit into common language the works of the Desert Fathers and other pioneers of our Christian faith, our children referred to my "dearest friends, most of whom had been dead for over a millennium!" While their irreverence was harmless fun, there was a grain of truth in their mischief. I was drawn to immerse myself in Augustine, John Chrysostom and the early Church Fathers, Bernard of Clairvaux and the monastic founders and later contemplatives like Theresa of Avila and John of the Cross. Lately, I have begun to wonder why it is that they have such wisdom for us that transcends the unrecognizable context in which we live today.

As I reread their texts and reflected quietly on what I knew of their lives and how they expressed their reality of a very Living God, I began to find myself drawn more deeply than ever into the refreshment of their wisdom. But why? Why were they getting my attention now, at 99, more deeply than ever before? I had studied them. They were the focus of my scholarship, yet I was knowing something more deeply than I had ever known it. It was all so new! Why did I sense their renewing influence in my seemingly "old" spirit? As I puzzled with this conundrum, I realized that this newness came because not only were they different from me and the scholarship I have engaged for most of my life, but that I now was different than I had been, and could hear and sense in new ways.

It is said, with some mischief, that the apex of authentic scholarship is realized when there are only one or two other people on the planet with whom you might enjoy a robust conversation! The microscopic mind formation of the scholar is to become more and more expert on less and less. The ancients, unburdened by the yet-undiscovered treasure trove of modern knowledge, peered through their intellectual telescopes backwards. As they looked into the mysteries of God, their vision grew wider, not narrower. Their minds were far less cluttered than ours. Like Mary, they chose only "one thing," to know Christ. Like my good friend, mentor and colleague in the formation of Regent, Marshall Sheppard, they adhered to the example of the Jewish scholar, now apostle Paul, "to know nothing while I was with you except Jesus Christ and him crucified" (1 Cor. 2:2). As I age, I must be satisfied with less and less, and yet it is becoming more and more!

So, not only were the ancients different, but I am different; first in my body, though not by choice, and as consequence in my mind, as well. Jesus affirmed Mary in her stillness, "she has chosen well." While I confess, I did not choose this state of being much more immobile than has been my life habit, it has forced me to see more, to go deeper, to be still with the deeper wisdom of the ancients and to hunger for what they had found in the greater simplicity with which they lived.

In consequence, the very disabling of what was once possible, is enabling a deeper reality of God than I have ever known and so, I find, I am "born again"...in my 100th year!

If ever we have all lived through a time when more of what we knew was upended by what is unknown and, for the most part, unwelcome, it is these past few years of pandemic. We can each produce litanies of things lost and longed for in "re-opening," or whatever lies ahead. My body will not "re-open" in the sense of new opportunity that many of you can sense ahead, and so my prayer for you is that—as you have opportunity to regain all the former "busyness" that may have been "stolen" by recent circumstances—you hold fast to this one thing: to know Christ, and Him crucified, and to treasure the path of Mary in resisting all the many new distractions that become possible, and retain a hunger for the few, even just the one thing—to know Christ and him crucified.

In friendship,

Jim

Section:

II

"Climbing Higher"

Letters Written from ...

March, 2022 – August, 2022

Psalm #2 of Jim (March, 2022 – August, 2022)

1) *Lord, I have discovered a park outside my window! When did You put that there? Trees—some ancient. A beach for swimming—Rita's beach—children playing outside, where my wheelchair can be pushed amidst the glorious sunshine of a summer's day!*

2) *Perhaps it was here all along. I just never noticed.*

3) *Back indoors, I watch the "regulars" as they pass my window. You know their stories, but I can imagine what they might be.*

4) *For one, the curved shoulders hint that their world is heavy. Another hides his habit just outside his door, banned from re-entry until the smoke has cleared. Another pushes a cart with all her worldly goods, in search of bottles that might magically be turned to coffee or even more.*

5) *Each story that walks by my window: You know them, Lord, right well, but how is it that mine seems so much more blessed? Why is it that I am still alive, more alive each day?*

6) *Lord, You hear the stories that are told inside, by visitors, by kind nurses and their aides, even the occasional doctor who is now far more occasional, and seemingly quite disinterested in any medical matters—of which I seem to offer so little these days.*

7) *How can I speak warmth into their too-cool hearts? Some burn for You, too few. Too many suffer quietly.*

8) And my friends keep dying, here and away. Mostly away. Will I, alone, be left? Do You really want me to be the very last of my generation? Do I really have to wait until they are all gone? Lord, I think You are helping me find something to do? Thank You!

9) Books seem to be arriving…O blessed Amazon, where else could I find obscure books that just arrive in their packages. It seems a new bookshelf is required. And here I thought I was done with books.

10) Letters go out and then they come in, as if the whole world were at my door, at this door, the one I wanted closed. It is so much better open. You have given me back a way to be with people. I thought I had lost it.

11) You have opened a way for communion, for voices from the past to speak their presence in the present. More visitors, too, come to say hello… after saying goodbye! Is this how You felt as you strode from the emptying tomb, as the Third Day unfolded?

12) It's little wonder that You ordained a Sabbath, not that I have ever found rest was easy. I think the friends who care for me could use one, a respite from the tide of visits that flood their front-door Covid testing, as each awaits entry to come and see me here.

13) Are You sending them, Lord? Some even fly from far away and fill my days with the wonder of life-long friendships. How blessed am I!

14) It was not so long ago that food meant a cup with a straw and some institutional gruel. How much better the emerging routine of a cup of glorious seafood soup and Caesar salad, by the beach, even on the beach, with the sounds of endless volleyball filling the summer air.

15) How thoughtful to put a restaurant so near my new home, for home it is—not a hospice place for dying, but a home for living, for even anticipating gravity upon awakening. Home for welcoming guests, as once Rita and I so loved. Home for looking at pictures on the wall, home for being very present to being alive.

16) Thank You, Lord. I think I might stay to turn 100, if You don't mind.

Letter #16

Editor's Note: As your scribe and Jim's son and editor, I write for Dad, to you, at a hard time. The peace for which many of Dad's generation gave their lives is under unprecedented assault in Ukraine. This letter will also herald the beginning of our Lenten season. As I write, it is the Sabbath, yet deeply uneasy. I have spoken with Dad about his own memories of the opening of the second war. They are bemusing, sobering but with much that does not seem relevant. I asked about this moment of time in our history, but the failures of telephony, deafness and growing confusion, left me bereft of clarity. So, I searched his recent notes to me—notes written at the beginning of this month—for what he might have to say for us all, now, on the brink of this profound unknowing about the future. Here, from one of Dad's best "friends" from the fifth century, Augustine of Hippo, comes a message of rest, Sabbath rest, that heralds the greatest hope of all, an eternity with God.

March 3, 2022

Dear friends,

As I search through the wisdom of the ancients and follow the thread of the seasons laid out in my own book of letters—*Letters of Faith Through the Seasons, Volume 1* (see pages 318-319)—I am reminded of what it means to know Sabbath rest. Though forced to less physical activity, my own mind is far from inactive, and I am as challenged as ever by the propensity to a busyness of soul that I still seek to be quieted.

In a letter to Januarius, thought to be Bishop of Benevento and later a martyr for his faith, Augustine of Hippo wrote concerning the Sabbath...

> For we are now, as I said above, living in exile in faith and hope, and what we are striving to attain by love is a certain holy and perpetual rest from all the toil of all our troubles. We have a passage from this life into it, a passage that our Lord Jesus Christ deigned to show us in advance and to make holy by his passion. In that rest, however, there is not a lazy idleness, but a certain ineffable tranquility of leisurely action. After all,

> we shall in the end rest from the works of this life so that we rejoice in the action of the next life. But because such action is carried out by the praise of God without the labor of our limbs and the worry of cares, we do not pass into that life through rest in such a way that toil takes its place, that is, so that the action of the next life does not begin so that our rest ceases.[6]

The "Sabbath" represented that original way of life, prior to the "Fall," on the seventh day. Afterwards, it was reinterpreted as "the Return of the Prodigal" now restored from wandering, accepted, and clothed in "the best robe," the spiritual "First Day of the Week," which we now call "The Lord's Day." When you read Genesis on the days of creation, you realize that originally the seventh day was now rest without end. But for the sinner, the original everlasting life was forfeited. Now "the first day of the week" represents a return to the original life, as everlasting rest, not forfeited but restored! ...

I know that these letters find you all over the world. Some are close and some far from this conflict that threatens to engulf it. I have vivid memories of *HMS Edinburgh,* at anchor in the Firth of Forth as war was declared in September 1939. A naval officer from the ship visited our home. We had no idea what his presence would come to represent. What lay ahead for us was beyond mere unknowing, it was unimaginable. And yet, the rise of a darkness that was to engulf Europe was also a rise in deepening dependence on the Living God. In the midst of darkness, the Light shines. In the midst of deep unease, Sabbath rest beckons.

I join Augustine in praying for you all… "You are great, Oh Lord, and greatly to be praised…You have made us for yourself, and our hearts are restless until they rest in you."[7] May each of you know the deep rest of our Living God in these days.

With my blessings and peace for each soul.

Your friend,

Jim

Letter #17

March 10, 2022

Dear friends,

For so much of my life I have been able to set the agenda for my days, to define the books I would read, lectures I would give, courses I would teach, students I would meet, projects that would consume me and timing that I would follow, as I was so inclined. To be sure, there were numerous obstacles, yet I recognize that the agenda was mine to set. It has taken running into the brick wall of aging and losing some faculties that render me dependent upon other people's timing to slow me down enough to ask, "What should I do next?" It is a question I have called my son Chris to ask on more than a few occasions, and I think we both find it disorienting to be in that place together. In it all, I have been helped by my own book of letters, not only because the content is helpful, but because it follows the church calendar. God has given us seasons of not only weather, but for our spirits. And now, we are in Lent.

The Lenten season offers us six Sundays and each has a focus, or an invitation to reflection. I think we might be wise to pay attention. Some years ago, I'm not sure I can remember just how many, I had been invited to speak at a Lenten conference on the subject, "The Celebration of Ash Wednesday." As I rose to my feet before speaking, unaware of the Anglican tradition of the community I was to address, I was given a charcoal cross on my forehead. As the son of an itinerant Brethren preacher, the "imposition of ashes," administered just before embarking on a message, was an interruption that I found both unusual and, upon reflection, prescient of the kinds of interruptions that would better prepare me for this stage of life. As we embark on even the best intentions, in our full stride, we need sometimes sharp reminders that our every breath comes at a huge cost, the cost of Christ's death for us.

I was fortunate in my first encounter with the sign of ashes, a sign I carried throughout my talk, that I was to speak about the Armenian Church, a church that has survived even the genocide at the hands of the Turks. In their tradition, Lent is the primary season of fasting among the 160 days of fasting assigned in their calendar. This time of reflection and of cleansing, of bodies and souls, prepares us to receive the gifts of Easter. This letter to you comes between the first and second Sundays of Lent. The first Sunday, now past, is our doorway into the Lenten season. In just a few days, we will meet the second Sunday that marks the expulsion of humanity from paradise and the loss of our happiness due to our disobedience. Later Sundays focus us elsewhere.

So, today, with limited capacity to set my own agenda and to find myself marked "figuratively," at least by imposed ashes, I am between two thresholds: my entry to Lent, and my expulsion from a paradise I rejected through disobedience, the first graciously offered by consequence of the second. I am welcomed to the Gift of Grace in spite of my choice otherwise, but I must enter through this Lenten gate not on my terms, but with purified feelings and renewed faith, welcoming Him who by His death defeated death and granted life to us by His resurrection. This is the gift of this season. It stops me in my tracks, insists on ashes for my face, so that I might enter more fully into the miracle of my salvation in Christ. That He should grant me another such season, a ninety-ninth, is cause of deep gratitude.

For you each I pray, "Grant, O Lord, to your faithful people—these dear friends of mine—that they enter the holy solemnities of this fast with true reverence and continue the same with steadfast devotion."

Welcome to your Lenten season!

Affectionately yours,

Jim

Letter #18

Editor's Note: Today, as I write, is the anniversary of Jim and Rita's wedding. They were married on March 20, 1953, in Glasgow, and a remarkable collaboration began. For those of you who knew Rita, our Mum, you will no doubt recall the uniquely "harmonious" way in which Jim and Rita found a grounded equilibrium between "heaven" and "earth." If Dad was a balloon in the sky, Mum was the anchor, rooted on the ground. That cable, which was their link for 60 years, preserved us all from too much sky or too much mud. Today, we honour their union.

During this Lenten season, Dad has written about Lent. He has told me of the Armenian Church and his visit with Archbishop Nerses Pozapalian, an encounter he describes in his notes as "the most remarkable Christian experience of my life." I can see Mum's eyebrows lifting, her throat being cleared to deliver in her broad Scots a point of view on Dad's choice of "remarkable experience"!??[8]

Today, March 20, 2022, a school was bombed in Mariupol. It is Lent, soon to Easter, and as your scribe I struggle to connect the bombed earth of today with my father's spiritual insight for our time. In honour of both Mum and Dad, this letter seeks a harmony that has nourished many of us for decades.

March 20, 2022

Dear friends,

Today is the third Sunday of Lent, in which we reflect upon the Prodigal Son. The Lenten days of fasting were established in the year 325, in Nicaea, at the first ecumenical council. Since then, the Armenian Church has annually dedicated 160 days to fasting, within which there is the "great fast" of forty days that Jesus himself practiced. This has always been a time to review one's deeds and behavior, just as an author reviews her text or an accountant his money. On this third Sunday, in the midst of the "great fast," we are invited to remember the son who found in his rebellion against his father a deep unhappiness, who "was lost, then found by his father," to help us learn how great is the Father's love for us; indeed, for all humankind.

In Old Testament times, the Lord called Israel with the call of a trumpet. Sometimes to celebrate. Sometimes to fast, or on occasion for war. The trumpet call was for serious occasions when a response was urgently required. "Blow a trumpet in Zion, declare a holy fast," says the prophet Joel (2:15). This warning signal calls us to fast in a holy manner, to take the moment very seriously, recognizing that God has pleasure in holy people, not just holy acts.

[Editor's note: In our childhood home, the sound of Mum clearing her throat, usually a harbinger of some withering phrase, was our "trumpet sound." It will echo for decades yet!]

Some twenty years ago, I was in Armenia and met with Archbishop Nerses Pozapalian who, at that time, had recently stepped away from an opportunity to be a candidate for the Catholicos—leader of the entire Armenian Church—encouraging his own former student to be elected instead. I was deeply moved by his story. Shortly after my visit, he wrote to me, including in his letter the exhortation that…

> "The present movement of the world is in turmoil, so we Christians have to find new ways and means to restore the desired tranquility to the world, in order that we may give hope and faith to the people of the world. Everywhere, secularization dominates over the churches and our communities. We must then have a special message for ordinary people."[9]

My encounter with this selfless leader has been the most remarkable Christian experience of my life. I was so moved by his renouncing of self-interest that I held his hand, as if I was in the presence of one of the Apostles. He seems to me Apostolic indeed, for his church originated only three centuries after Pentecost! My own journey through such renouncing came less through my choice and more by the choice of others, when I lost my role as Principal of Regent College. This time was for me a deep, dark night of the soul. A time when, like the prodigal, I could only throw myself helplessly into the arms of my heavenly Father. I was stripped of all the dignity I cherished and yet, in His mercy, He placed new robes on me, and led me into a life in the classroom with students and with the ancient saints in the cloister.

This is our calling as followers of Jesus in this time of "the great fast": to give up far more than mere chocolate, or even fine wine, but to yield up our pride, our demand for our will, to relinquish our place to another, to even be emptied. Our gracious Lord calls us to this place uniquely, even tenderly, but relentlessly, for such is His love.

Today is the anniversary of my marriage to my dear Rita. I miss her and yet we are so close, for the veil that separates us grows thinner by the day. Some days, when I had invited yet more guests to our home than perhaps I had remembered to tell Rita, I found myself with the prodigal son, "sent to Coventry" as the English might say! And yet, our covenant ran deep. She loved me fiercely. And she loved her Lord and His Word. How much more, though, we are each welcomed as the "prodigal," when we come empty to our Heavenly Father's heart. In this Lenten season, may you each know His warm welcome upon your return.

Affectionately yours,

Jim

Letter #19

Editor's Note: On occasion, the notes from Dad that inspire your scribe in editing these letters contain threads that are hard for lesser mortals to fathom. Today, oranges, mystics, introspection and scurvy conspire to make the search for exegetical connections rather hard to fathom. I trust that I have indeed found the golden thread to link them all and grasp coherence for us all from the sometimes-mysterious wisdom of a sage!

March 24, 2022

Dear friends,

Soon, we will encounter the fourth Sunday in Lent. This Sunday is dedicated to the encounter of Jesus with the rich young ruler, whom he sent away to reflect on the real state of his eager heart. His challenge, from Jesus, was to find renewal in his life through the abandonment of the very competence by which he thought he was being successful. The reality is we cannot "fix" ourselves but must first be emptied of that upon which we have depended for our sense of self.

I grew up in Spain as the son of missionary parents. My mother, who served near the small town of Avila before I was born, was there introduced to its famous saint, Theresa. My mother grew to love her writings. My father, meanwhile, introduced me to a peer and perhaps inspiration for Theresa, John of Avila. John had studied law at Salamanca and biblical studies at the new biblical institute of Alcala, and he planned to serve as missionary in Mexico. Ill health forced him to live a more restricted life, devoted to letter writing.

Were it not for scurvy on British merchant ships, I may never have met this remarkable Franciscan through his writings, and in particular, his letter to a young lady about the dangers of excessive introspection. You see, English ships gathered oranges from Spain to offset the risks of scurvy across the navy. These English ships travelled to eager readers, which led to the translation of John of Avila's letters into English. Thus, they came to my father's hands and thence to me. On the subject of introspection and action—the challenging standard that Jesus set for the rich young ruler—John of Avila wrote to his friend…

> How long will you continue in your minute self-examinations? It is like raking up a dust heap from which nothing can come but rubbish and unpleasantness. Feel sure that it is not for your own merits, but for those of Christ crucified, that you are loved and made whole. Do not give way to such discouragement about your faults. It would be far better to be courageous and strong-hearted and to meditate on the benefits that you have received through Jesus Christ in the past and possess now…As I have often repeated, God loves you as you are…what more have you to wish for? In heaven, there is one to whom you appear all fair for He looks at you through the apertures of the wounds that he received for you. By these he gives you grace and supplies what is lacking in you, healing you and making you lovely. Be at peace![10]

Like the young ruler in the encounter with Jesus, John of Avila found himself unable to "do" enough to warrant his own sense of merit. John was stuck in bed when he longed to be a missionary in Mexico. The young man who encountered Jesus had already done all he could think of, yet he sensed it was still not enough. And John, in his letter, invites his friend to embrace her adequacy in Christ, not her inadequacy in her own eyes. In a way, I now understand the perspective of John of Avila, that it is through an emptied self, a self so constrained that Christ is able to work more fully. These letters to you, my friends, are part of that journey for me. May you each, in your own hearts, respond with gratitude for the high place you hold in God's heart, and set aside your inability to make your own self righteous.

My prayer for you this week is, "May God's mercy shelter you beneath His everlasting love and for this, I bid you hope." Please pray also for me, the same, and to the same Lord, who loves us all.

Affectionately yours,

Jim

Letter #20

March 31, 2022

Dear friends,

Next Sunday, the fifth Sunday in Lent, is set aside by my friends in the ancient Armenian church as the Sunday of the "Unjust Judge," a reference to the parable that Jesus told that is recorded in Luke 18:1-8. In other traditions, the text is referred to as the parable of the "persistent widow." As is so often the case, perspective is everything. And at a time when everywhere and everything seems more discouraging than hopeful, I am challenged to reflect on how we are invited to deal with our perhaps very legitimate discouragement, concerning the state of both our own affairs and especially, perhaps, those of the world. Through this parable, we are encouraged to pray and not lose heart. It reminds me of a time when losing heart seemed to me a much more sensible interpretation of events!

While I am generally not given to depression, there was a time when I think I understood, for a while, what countless others experience as a deep blackness from which no light escapes or breaks in. In the very early days of Regent, we had emigrated as a family from Oxford with our four children, then in their early teens. My brother-in-law was most displeased because I had taken his sister away from her family "to another continent." My fellow Christian leaders were displeased because we were pursuing a "trans-denominational" character and eschewing the preferences of any one denomination. A well-intentioned "Job's comforter" told me as he resigned that I had made a huge mistake if the college went bankrupt, but that I could at least count on a land of opportunity for my children! The various Christian voices concerning what Regent should become had become a veritable "Tower of Babel" and to cap it all off, the University Senate was on the verge of rejecting our affiliation request. Only our brave faculty seemed "on side."

As I look back on this period, I have this sense of having risked all and looking into an abyss of God's abandonment. There appeared no solid reason to think that I had not made a disastrous mistake. I could not go forward, and I had no way back. I felt miserably trapped by it all. All I remember praying was "Lord, though [you] slay me, yet will I hope in [you]" (Job 13:15). It was not a prayer of real hope, just one of resignation, of deep dependence, of abandonment—not to despair, but into the arms of Christ. I trusted because, like the disciples, I had nowhere else to go.

As we know, the story of Regent that follows has a "happy ending." But that was not the reality of my discouragement in those darkest of days. My reality was that all was coming apart, that it seemed nothing was about to work together for good. My son Chris has asked me to reflect on what provided encouragement at this stage of my life. I have answered his question, not with a theory of encouragement, but with this experience of deep discouragement. To really know encouragement, we have to know despair, to know a coming to the end of ourselves that is so complete, so absorbing, that we find we have nowhere else to go but to our knees.

Chris and I share a precious memory of a time when our youngest child, Jonathan, was struggling for his life, in the years before we came to Regent and Vancouver. Chris, then in his early teens, found me late one night, weeping in prayer in our living room in Oxford, wrestling over a decision on whether to operate to seek to save the life of our young son with Down's Syndrome. His survival would change the life of our family irrevocably. Immigration to Canada would have been impossible. Together, Chris and I wept before the Lord, recognizing that ours was to choose life, and live in and on the mercy of God. Again, with the disciples we prayed "Lord, to whom can we go!" The Lord took Jonathan home. Years later, dear Rita met a surgeon's wife who recounted how her husband had fought to save our Jonathan's life, only to see it slip from his skilled grasp.

Over our years of friendship, many of you have shared with me the stories of your own deep discouragement. To be at the end of ourselves, at the end of our hope, is but a part of what it means to be truly human. What we learn at those moments defines how and where we seek encouragement in the years that follow. As I reflect on my own life, I see these defining moments of deep despair as just that: defining. They have shaped me. Through them God has molded me, even changed me so that even now, when so much that I would love to do is not possible, I am content. "Lord, though [you] slay me, yet will I hope in [you]" (Job 13:15). The widow in Christ's parable persisted, even against the unjust judge, and so must we.

With great certainty I pray for each of you, that our lives—that your lives—would embody the exhortation of the apostle, encouraging one another and building one another up.

Affectionately yours,

Jim

Letter #21

April 4, 2022

Dear friends,

As we approach this last Sunday of Lent before Easter, we need to do so with some trepidation. In the events of Palm Sunday, we see the crowds enthralled by Jesus as He rode into the city. In no time, their praise turned to jeers and cries of "Crucify Him, Crucify Him!" How quickly they turned. How weak their certainty in Messiah. How soon I find that I follow their lead and find my faith too shallow. It is so easy for us to become "habitual Christians," to find ourselves in a kind of dream-walk where we have stopped choosing our faith as a daily rigour and it has become stale and motionless. We have stopped walking by faith and we have simply sat down—for too long.

This past week has been a precious milestone for me in a very tangible way. As I have written before, my arrival at this care hospital came about as a result of a fall in my apartment where I remained alone on the floor for many hours. It was a frightening time, and I found that I could no longer take care of enough of my needs, and so was very fortunate to find a space at this beautiful care hospital. Slowly but surely, the physical trainers *[Editor's note: Dad calls them his "gymnasts"–we try to keep a straight face!]* have been pushing me to walk again and this week, for the first time in nearly a year, I walked without support, back to my room and settled in my "writing" chair. It might not have been much, but for me, it was a triumph. I was delighted to call my children and tell them of my recovery.

[Editor's Note: While his children are delighted at Dad's new-found mobility, we now no longer have the same assurance that we know what he gets up to, in light of his rather vigorous spirit of independence!]

This simple act of walking again, which I have been fortunate enough to re-discover, is precisely the kind of reorientation, or widening, of being aroused, in a very tangible way from a "sleep" of habitual faith, to which our Lenten reflection calls us. Just as I am reminded through the simple act of locomotion of what it means to be more fully alive, so we need to become more conscious of all the riches that we have in Christ. As Jesus walked with his face set towards Jerusalem, as He chose life for us, so we are invited to choose Life, vibrant, full-on, one-foot-in-front-of-the-other living! Just as Jesus exhorted Nicodemus, so we each need to be "born again," to be re-captivated by the miracle of our identity in Christ, to actually live as if our lives have been redeemed. Imagine, we have been made anew! We are new creatures! For me, at 99, the simple act of walking across a room—something I have not done for nearly a year—is a glorious act of being reborn to walking! How much more do we each need to be re-born to our wearied and even lost faith. To the man at the Pool of Bethesda, Jesus said so distinctly, "pick up your mat and walk" (John 5:8)!

In the evangelical tradition where the "sermon is all," we often miss the hymns. I love many hymns! These poems of our faith, like the psalms, have been my precious companions these days. I can remember them. How fitting for this season of new birth is one of my favourites...

> Be Thou my vision, O Lord of my heart.
> Naught be all else to me, save that Thou art.
> Thou my best thought, by day or by night;
> Waking or sleeping, Thy presence my light.
>
> Be Thou my wisdom, and Thou my true word.
> I ever with Thee and Thou with me, Lord.
> Thou my great Father, and I Thy true son
> Thou in me dwelling and I with Thee one.
>
> High King of heaven, my victory won.
> May I reach heaven's joys, O bright heaven's sun
> Heart of my own heart, whatever befall
> Still be my vision, O ruler of all.[11]

This hymn is also a favourite of my 2 ½ year-old granddaughter, Addie, whose daddy sings it to her before all her sleeps. She and I have this in common. Perhaps you can find it helpful too. May the Lord meet you as you are still before Him. May he refresh your tired spirits. May you learn to leap again in your hearts of faith and let Christ's vision and presence be yours.

Affectionately yours,

Jim

Letter #22

April 11, 2022

Dear friends,

The remarkable events of Easter will soon be upon us, and I find that I approach these special moments in the Christian calendar with a question: "Is this my last?" While we all live with the reality of such questions, I find it more tangible. Yet with each day, my sense of completion grows ever deeper. It is good. It is in the way of things and as Good Friday beckons, I find that I can better enter into Christ's deep sleep of dependence upon His Father, even the sleep of His death.

In the past weeks, I have been finding that moment between wakefulness and sleep to be filled with music. Whether I am dreaming and realizing the dream, or in a kind of reverie, I don't know. I'm not sure that matters much. But I keep hearing a hymn that was one of my father's favourites, "The Day Thou Gavest Lord is Ended." I hear it as being sung sweetly by angels. Their voices move me to tears. I wonder where comes these melodies.

It was later in his life that my own father drew to my attention his love for this hymn. It intrigues me that it so comes to me late in my own life. My father and I did not see all eye to eye. Far from it. My last remembrance of him is having a debate about the role of music in worship. There we were, father and son, on a train platform, arguing. It was my last earthly remembrance of him. And yet, here I am some 63 years since I last spoke with him audibly, hearing him now. These words have become like a pillow, inviting me to lay down my head. So close. So dear. I just want to sleep, to respond to the Lord's invitation to dwell with him eternally. And I catch a faint glimpse not only of the suffering Christ, but the trusting Christ as he cried out, "into your hands I commit my spirit" (Luke 23:46). I am thankful for this rehearsal in the quietness of my room. Here is this hymn that beckons my sleep…

The day you gave us, Lord, is ended,
The darkness falls at your request;
To you our morning hymns ascended,
Your praise shall sanctify our rest.

We thank you that your Church, unsleeping
While earth rolls onward into light,
Through all the world her watch is keeping
And never rests by day or night.

As over continent and island
Each dawn leads to another day,
The voice of prayer is never silent,
Nor do the praises die away.

So be it, Lord! Your throne shall never,
Like earth's proud empires, pass away;
Your kingdom stands and grows forever
'til all thy creatures own thy sway.[12]

The theme of this hymn, special to me—and to my father before me, and I hope an encouragement to you—echoes Psalm 113:3, "From the rising of the sun to the place where it sets, the name of the Lord is to be praised." It echoes the command recorded in Genesis that out of darkness the light shall come, and it reflects the vision of John in Revelation 5:13, "every creature in heaven and on earth and under the earth and on the sea, and all that is in them, saying: "To him who sits on the throne and to the Lamb be praise and honor and glory and power, for ever and ever!""

I know of nothing quite so trusting as to fall asleep, to yield consciousness to the One who holds our identity secure in His knowing of us. The darkness falls at His request...but so does the Light come forth! As He is Risen, so shall we each one day. That is why this sweet pillow of praise comforts so. May it be for each of you also. Happy Easter!

With resurrection hope!

Jim

Letter #23

April 21, 2022

Dear friends,

Each day, in the endless patterns of our daily routine in this home, my floor is swept. It never strikes me that it much needs sweeping, but that is what happens each day. Recently, on a day so much like any other, I was watching the face of the lovely girl who daily sweeps my clean floor. She looked so sad. I think I would have been sad if my life had revolved around sweeping a floor that seemed clean, but on this day, Sandra—for that is her name—impressed me with a deeper sadness than I had seen before. And so I asked, "Why so tired and so sad?" And thereupon, with broom in hand, large tears fell from her eyes to moisten the clean floor at her feet. My new friend Sandra wept.

There is a close community of nurses and caregivers in our hospital. They are largely of one ethnic community and profess one faith. There are few exceptions. Sandra is one, from the same ethnic community but professing another faith, and her sense of isolation and loneliness was breaking her heart. She is not alone. As our global population rises, alienation has become epidemic. Never were we closer together physically, yet never further apart relationally. This pandemic, ever the accelerant of so many changes, has driven us behind doors, behind masks, behind even our own faces, to inhabit fear alone. Sandra, pushing her broom amidst all the denizens of our hospital floors, found herself weeping with me as I recounted for her the lines of George Herbert in his poem "The Elixir"... "A servant with this cause, makes drudgery divine: who sweeps a room, as for thy laws, makes that and th' action fine."[13]

Before Sandra came in that day, I had been reading in Ephesians 2:10, "For we are God's handiwork." When the eternal Father sent His Son, He sent Him in a peasant girl's womb, whose husband was later a carpenter. Jesus, with His father Joseph, made yokes for oxen so fields could be cultivated, grain could be harvested, so bread could be made, so that people could eat. The economy of the whole village depended on the yokes made for oxen. Years later, Jesus was to preach, "Take my yoke upon you...and you will find rest for your souls" (Matt. 11:29). Jesus made good yokes. They mattered. But my friend and floor sweeper, on this day, only sensed her alienation, both social and professional. She could not even claim the professional merit of being a nurse. Events had conspired to leave her separated from others on every dimension of importance to her. And her broom, though vital to our clean hospital, was of no comfort.

Sadly, our culture, often our Christian culture, has linked identity and work, or our profession, far too closely. As an academic, I know this trap all too well: "Who I am and my sense of belonging derives from my performance." This is the lie that Christ destroyed on the cross of Easter. In that moment, He forever rooted worth, our worth, the significance of my new friend Sandra, not in performance, but in Love. We are all Sandras, all floor-sweepers, all doing not enough for merit, all alien from one another, until the Cross of Easter fulfills every letter of the law, and we are made whole. May the prayer of George Herbert guide our hearts hungry for significance and belonging.

> Teach me, my God and King,
> In all things Thee to see,
> And what I do in anything
> To do it as for Thee.
>
> Not rudely, as a beast,
> To run into an action;
> But still to make Thee prepossest,
> And give it his perfection.
>
> ...
>
> This is the famous stone

That turneth all to gold;
For that which God doth touch and own
Cannot for less be told.[14]

With my prayers that all your "floor-sweeping" bring you joy as you do all for the Lord.

With my blessings,

Jim

Letter #24

April 28, 2022

Dear friends,

I have been reflecting this past week, as I triumph in my recovered ability to walk, that there exists a crushing injustice of which, at 99, I am a most unworthy beneficiary. My life has been full, mostly safe, extraordinarily fulfilling, rich in mercies and people and memories—and now I am enjoying immensely the renewed pleasures of simply walking around a table, down hallways, greeting many friends, old and new. Yet at the very same time, as an immeasurably blessed old man in Vancouver relishes in the spring sunshine, harmless young men and children are gunned down, bombed out of their homes, driven to flee for their lives…if they are the lucky ones. The dissonance in all this stuns me into incomprehension and numbs my ability to even process what I see and hear. Yet numbness is the very quality I reject so vigorously, even as it helps me cope.

Some years ago, I came across this hymn, which perhaps better than many frames my cry to the Lord as I resist ambivalence—yet cannot comprehend the scale of misery in Ukraine. The words of this hymn, which dates from the 1980s, were written by Shirley Murray. She said, "I wrote it for Amnesty International's campaign against torture when I could not find anything relevant to sing at a service for Prisoners of Conscience." Please join me in this prayer of my heart…

> God of freedom God of justice
> You whose love is strong as death
> You who saw the dark of prison
> You who knew the price of faith
> Touch our world of sad oppression
> With Your Spirit's healing breath
>
> Rid the earth of torture's terror

You whose hands were nailed to wood
Hear the cries of pain and protest
You who shed the tears and blood
Move in us the power of pity
Restless for the common good

Make in us a captive conscience
Quick to hear to act to plead
Make us truly sisters brothers
Of whatever race or creed
Teach us to be fully human
Open to each other's needs.[15]

We all live daily with this sharp dissonance between ways in which we are blessed and ways in which others suffer. Just sometimes, that dissonance reaches a crescendo when we seem so powerless to affect a different outcome, except to open our homes and our wallets and share of what we have unreasonably received. I am reminded to reach deeper into my capacity for gratitude, to invite the Lord to further enlarge my heart, to make me a captive of conscience and so be open to another's needs, here amidst the hurting hearts in this lovely hospital.

May the Lord make clear to each of you in what ways
He would have you reflect His compassionate heart.

Jim

Letter #25

May 5, 2022

Dear friends,

It is a few weeks past Easter. Now, for most of us, it is but a past date in our calendar. Easter was a passing moment, a *then*. We think of it as an event, historical, a commemoration, something past. In our packed and racing lives in which we so often turn "being busy" into a badge of honour, Easter is already long fading into the blur of our rear-view mirrors. Yet, "Easter" is more than just a noun. It is also a verb, an action, capable of being past, present and future. Not that we think of it that way...but we should.

Gerard Manley Hopkins, in his epic poem "The Wreck of the Deutschland," in which he commemorates the death of five nuns at sea, ends his intricate recounting of a tragedy with a prayer...

> Let him easter in us, be a dayspring to the dimness of us, be a crimson-cresseted east,
> More brightening her, rare-dear Britain, as his reign rolls,
> Pride, rose, prince, hero of us, high-priest,
> Our hearts' charity's hearth's fire, our thoughts' chivalry's throng's Lord.[16]

Hopkins captures my attention with his plea, "let him easter in us... be a day-spring to the dimness in us." It is as if as we race through our calendars away from the event of Easter, we need to let the resurrection moment, miracle, marvel, triumph, not to fade but to stay with us, to catch us in our fleeing down the months and burst forth day-spring in the dimness of us. We are eastered by the light bursting over the horizon before us, of an east that we never reach but yet run toward. For the resurrection of Christ has created an unimaginable present and future for us. To be eastered is to enter a new heaven on earth, to live not only in the past event of the resurrection but in its triumphant future. Our being eastered is not only past, but it is also now, and it lies ahead.

The "eastered" poet Isaac Watts wrote this poem:

> I'll praise my Maker while I've breath,
> and when my voice is lost in death,
> praise shall employ my nobler powers.
> My days of praise shall ne'er be past
> while life and thought and being last,
> or immortality endures.
>
> Happy are those whose hopes rely
> on Israel's God, who made the sky,
> the earth and seas, with all their train.
> This truth for ever stands secure:
> God saves the oppressed, God feeds the poor,
> and none shall find this promise vain.
>
> The Lord gives eyesight to the blind;
> the Lord supports the fainting mind,
> and sends the troubled conscience peace.
> God helps the stranger in distress,
> the widow and the fatherless,
> and grants the prisoner sweet release.
>
> I'll praise you while you lend me breath,
> and, when my voice is lost in death,
> praise shall employ my nobler powers.
> My days of praise shall ne'er be past,
> while life and thought and being last,
> or immortality endures.[17]

As you may notice, I am finding great comfort in the companionship of those that have gone before, in the "communion of saints." Some weeks ago, I told my son Chris that I felt as Pilgrim, from Bunyan's *Pilgrim's Progress,* now standing on the banks of the river, looking across at the celestial city. So much, nearly all, of my journey lies behind. I have but a short way to go. Chris asked me to describe the view ahead that was mine through these eyes that have peered forward for nearly one hundred years. I find it hard to describe, but perhaps one sense is this gathering of God's people, in worship, through these hymns that I have shared. Perhaps I am letting the event of Easter, which I have so often raced past, catch up with me, embrace me, allowing myself to be "eastered," to be so infused with the wonder of Christ's resurrection that it shapes my view of everything and praise. Joining the "communion of saints" is my inevitable response.

My friends, I cannot know the events of your days, yet in the midst of what seems urgent, I pray that you may find space to allow an Easter that now seems past to catch up with your busyness. May you allow the resurrected Christ to easter you, to draw you into the wonder of his forever presence, and so to bring your hearts to praise.

With my blessing upon your eastered hearts,

Jim

Letter #26

May 12, 2022

Dear friends,

In my letter of last week, I introduced the notion of Easter not just as a noun that referred to an event, but also as a verb by which we can "be eastered," to yield ourselves to the remarkable transformation brought about by the resurrection of Christ. It seems that we are always facing change and transition and so look for anything of permanence that might hold fast while all about is changed. Every generation faces disturbing transitions.

In recent weeks I had the pleasure of living vicariously through trips that two of my children have made to the land of my childhood, Scotland, and in particular, the city of Edinburgh. About two centuries ago, the city of Edinburgh was in great turbulence as it emerged from the Reformation with its "noble martyrs" to the Scottish Enlightenment. In the then-farm fields below the old city on its hill, a "New Town" was emerging. Two worlds, "Old Town" and "New Town," moving in parallel, yet so different one from another. It was a time of vibrant experimentation in philosophy, in architecture, in medicine, in maritime exploration—the findings of Captain Cook were heralding a whole new world. Very little that the grand city of Edinburgh knew was stable. Experiments in faith abounded, and the dour and rational Scots were challenged to trust God even with their emotions.

Two centuries later, somehow nothing has changed. As the post-WWII geopolitical peace crumbles in Ukraine and the Far East; as inflationary forces stifle our debt-fueled growth; as the authority of medicine is both embraced and challenged for global human health; as climate change threatens an already fragile food supply; as post-pandemic mental health issues rattle the composure of nearly all of us and tear at the fabric of already vulnerable families, none of us is immune from the growing sense that all our foundations are rattling, if not in tectonic flux. Where on earth is there any "solid ground" for our too-fragile selves?

Two centuries ago, in the midst of an epochal change in my old home-town of Edinburgh, Robert Smith published his first version of *Sacred Music,* a compilation of hymns appropriate for his charge as precentor and choirmaster of St George's, as he selected the hymns that his congregation needed. Amongst his choices was a hymn written as a paraphrase of Psalm 34 over a century previously, by Nicholas Brady and Nahum Tate in their *New Version of the Psalms* (1698). Their desire is mine also: to bring afresh the ancient texts of the Psalms to speak to us in a world unimagined by previous generations. Now, over three centuries later, this evergreen poem—which interprets Psalm 34, a psalm of David spoken out of a fear that led to his feigned madness before Abimelech—captures the essence of our times of upheaval and frames my response to the random chaos that seems to threaten our familiar order.

> Through all the changing scenes of life, in trouble and in joy,
> The praises of my God shall still my heart and tongue employ...
>
> O magnify the Lord with me, with me exalt his name;
> When in distress, to him I called. He to my rescue came.
> The hosts of God encamp around the dwellings of the just;
> His saving help he gives to all who in his mercy trust.
>
> O taste his goodness, prove his love; experience will decide
> How blessed they are, and only they, who in his truth confide.
> Fear him, you saints, and you will then have nothing else to fear;
> His service shall be your delight, your needs shall be his care.
>
> To Father, Son and Spirit, praise! To God whom we adore
> Be worship, glory, power and love, both now and evermore!

To be "eastered" is to yield to the incomprehensible mastery of all circumstances by a resurrected Christ. It is to descend into what may seem like madness to those around you. It is to taste his goodness, prove his love, and confide in his truth. A truth that has stood for millennia and will surely weather these uncertain days. May you each be so eastered as we exalt his name together.

With my blessings,

Jim

Letter #27

Editor's note: The following letter was derived from a brief conversation that Dad and your scribe enjoyed as he reflected upon our attendance at the Regent Convocation of 2022. As usual, adherence thematically has been achieved while adding a touch of Rita's "humour" to the otherwise somber moment!

May 19, 2022

Dear friends,

Last week, on Monday evening, I enjoyed a special moment. Two of my children accompanied me to the Convocation of graduates for Regent College. While I did not stay for it all, I managed the first part and it was a treat. I remember our first, over fifty years ago. There were more faculty than graduating students. I think some people thought we had rather over-extended on gowns and regalia and should have waited until we had a more robust student body. We did the right thing at the time, living into an unknown future to "be" who we "were not yet." While graduations and convocations seem to celebrate the accomplishments of graduands who become graduates by meeting the credentialling standards of the academic institution, I think of them as a celebration of a completely unknowable future, and so, its warm embrace.

It was my pleasure on Monday last to sit next to my friend Cindy. On this occasion, we were sort of dressed alike. Her shoes were different from the wide felt slippers that are my daily footwear, and she sat in a chair and not the wheel-chair that had allowed me to roll in next to her, but our robes were identical. The colours of our gowns matched perfectly though earned more than a half-century apart. Cindy likely bought her gown, as I did, from Shepherd and Woodward, on the High Street, in Oxford, who have been selling academic regalia for over 150 years and from whom Rita and I also bought school uniforms for our children. I remember buying my gown in the late 1940s. I did not buy the hat. I couldn't afford it at the time, and have managed well enough without it since. My gown is a lot more frayed and worn than that of my friend and colleague Cindy, and when I wore it for the first time, I walked across the stage to receive my degree with an eye on a future that now, having lived just about all of it, I realize was completely unknowable at the time.

Likewise today, as our students walked on stage as graduands and left the stage as graduates, peering ahead into the total fog of an unknowable future, I am reminded once again of what it means to live by faith and not by sight. While convocation seems centred on lauding the academic accomplishments of the students, that pales in the tacit assumption of just how much future lies ahead for each celebrant. At 99, I have pretty good recollection of virtually the entirety of my future as I could not see it in 1947. Then, the war was over. I had not met Rita. I had not been to Canada. I had not thought of "spiritual theology." I did not know that most of my future literary friends had already been dead for centuries. As for my future, I knew virtually nothing at all, as it turns out. I might have seen my way across the stage to collect my DPhil, but I was blind as a bat, as Rita would have put it. And so it is for us all.

Today, as I write, we face an equally unknowable future. While that seems pretty obvious, a great deal of effort goes into trying to read the "tea leaves," prognosticating and otherwise replacing as much as possible of the unknowable with the reasonably imagined. Pundits abound; most are wrong. For the most part, peering forward doesn't work. Even when I have tried (many times) to anticipate what lies ahead, I am left with only one certainty—and that is the character of faithfulness of our God. So, rather than knowing, we find ourselves simply believing that He who began a good work in us will complete it, though we have no idea how. I am somewhat bemused when I violate the very principle I am here espousing and consider what may lie ahead for us all. For a lifetime, as a scholar and as a Christian academic, I have pursued the scholarship of the mind. Our industrialized world has leveraged our capacity to reason, to think, to turn ideas into technology, to capitalize on the left brain. Our future, however, will likely be marked by the maturing of our understanding of our emotions and the integration of mind with heart. The future that I once could never see but have now lived will not come again. Were I to walk across that stage again, to step brightly into a new but still unknowable future, I am sure I would have walked a very different path yet found that each step was walked with the same very faithful God, the same yesterday, today and tomorrow. I find myself excited for our recent graduates, not because of what they have so diligently learned, important as that may be, but for the future revealing of that which they do not know at all, could never know at this point, but upon whom they can be quite certain. For, like Paul, I know whom I have believed, and am fully persuaded that He is able to keep that which has been committed to His care.

My prayer for you each, this day, is that you graduate into the child-like faith that alone can bring certainty as we each walk into unknown and unknowable days.

Fondly, and with my blessing,

Jim

Letter #28

Editor's Note: In the fall of 2021, I sat with Dad during a prolonged hospital stay. We were discussing his death: its likely imminence, his enthusiasm for rest from the weariness of body that had overtaken him and, naturally enough, the arrangements for funerals and memorial services and other related matters. It was challenging and a hard conversation, but not overly so, just something that needed to be done well. As it turned out, Dad and Mark Twain had much in common as rumors of death turned out to be much exaggerated! Nonetheless, during our conversation, Dad had said that, instead of the customary photograph at the "front of the church," near the casket, he wanted a copy of Psalm 1. I asked Dad for his reasoning and what, apart from the obvious disruption of tradition that he rather favours, he might be wanting to convey by such a choice.

In more recent weeks, Dad has been drawn back, once again, to the Psalms, which will serve as our focus for the next few letters. The gateway to the Psalter is Psalm 1, and in light of Dad's request regarding his memorial service—should it occur in my lifetime or yours!—we begin this series with an understanding of what Dad sees in this significant first Psalm. You will also find a new piece of calligraphy prepared by Tim Botts on the inside of the rear cover, which your scribe recently commissioned, to serve later as Dad requested. Tim's beautiful rendition captures the essence of Dad's sense of the Psalm's meaning, for him.

May 26, 2022

Dear friends,

Our entry into the Psalter is Psalm 1, which begins with this simple word "Blessed." The Psalm is a doorway to the psalter, but it is much more. It is a doorway to a life path, a doorway to two fundamental choices, to a fruitful life or a life characterised by "chaff." The psalm has echoes of the Genesis garden, of tree with fruit, some welcome and some forbidden. There are limits. As we are bound by the choices of Adam and Eve, so our and others' lives become bound by our choices. For some, this combination of blessings and curses that we find in this psalm are a problem. The language of the psalmist is harsh, uncompromising. It draws sharp distinctions and harkens to a memory of expulsion from an Edenic garden.

As inheritors of this ontological garden place of Adam, we all find that the choices reflected in this first Psalm are before each of us. What will characterize our lives? What path am I still on, even now, as nearly all my life is behind me? I find the first Psalm to be like a diamond with many facets. I can see it as a proverb that reveals what is wise or foolish. It reminds me of the parable of the wise and foolish virgins who waited, some to find they had enough oil and some to find they had run out. Last year, I thought that I had run out of oil. I hoped that I had. I wanted to go "home," but the Lord had more life for me to live, so I find I must not run out of oil too soon!

The psalm also seems like biography to me, for it tells two narratives, of some who live wisely and of some who choose not to and have a horrible death. Daily, I must still decide which road I want to take. Sometimes, it seems like a guidebook for a lifelong pilgrimage where we stop on the way many, many times and ask "which way to go" or "which road to take." For me, this first psalm still helps me choose daily a proverb, a biography, a pilgrim path. I am reminded of Holman Hunt's famous painting that hangs in Keble College chapel, in Oxford, of Christ, with the lamp, and His thorn-rimmed brow, at the door. Evangelically, the painting is interpreted as Christ knocking at the door of our heart, but I prefer to go far beyond that mere beginning of "I believe" to anticipate Christ's promise: "I go and prepare a place for you" (John 14:3). I embrace Jerome's analogy of the psalms as a vast mansion and so, this first psalm is our door, a lantern-lit entrance, with Christ my guide. I hope you will come with me to venture within. I like the way my friend Mark Anderson has paraphrased the Psalm in his poem, "The Choice."

How blessed are those
who don't follow the advice of the self-seeking,
subscribe to their twisted values
or join in their empty sneering.
They delight instead in following Yahweh's law.
Drawing on its wisdom day and night,

they thrive like trees beside clear flowing streams
bearing fruit without pause,
growing old but not weak
and flourishing, always flourishing.

But not the self-seeking!
They're like tumbleweed in the wind.
Without a leg to stand on before God's law
they find no place among his people.
Because God stakes out the path
of those who please him
while the road the wicked choose
leads to doom and disaster.[18]

Next week, I will share further the richness of this psalm with particular reference to the beautiful work by Tim Botts that now hangs in my room before my bed. I hope you can enjoy this vibrant image and let it speak to you a welcome as we enter in and learn to "sing a new song" with the Psalter, together.

In friendship,

Jim

Letter #29

Editor's Note: The following reflection is derived from a three-way interaction between Dad and your scribe and then with Tim Botts, as Tim prepared this rendition of Psalm 1. We would like to connect the visual with the insight that lies behind Tim's art. The themes and reflections are from Dad and Chris; the beauty and wise visual interpretation is from Tim.

June 2, 2022

Dear friends,

For generations, God's people, especially in hardship, have turned to the Psalms. At this moment, pandemics, "hot wars" in Europe, oil and food price shocks, to mention but a few, seem quite enough reasons to search for some comfort in the chaos. Yet for many of us, Psalm 1, the gateway to the psalter, is rocky ground on whose hard words we hurt our feet, with sounds that do not resonate in our ears. Much of its language is discordant, uncomfortable, even overly harsh for our politically corrected ears. We are greeted in its early verses by the "counsel of the wicked," the "way of sinners," and the "seat of scoffers." Then, after a brief interlude, we are sent on our way with "chaff which the wind drives away," and more "wicked," more "sinners," and new judgement, all building to a climax in the dire prediction that "the wicked will perish." Surrounded as we are by pandemic-induced chaos, geopolitical turmoil, and a seething form of PTSD that seems to have strangled us all in some way or another, why would I ever bother to pick up the psalter, if this is how I am greeted? And yet, through this wasteland of discouragement and even deep discord, a river of life runs.

A river is only a river if there is a valley, if there are mountains between which it can meander, if at the edge of its vibrant flow, there are dark and even dirty banks. The river is only a river when it is not the surrounding landscape, when it carves its way through the rocky detritus that it may itself have uncovered from the earth. In the centre of this psalm is the metaphor of tree and river. As if hearkening back to the precious but remote first word "Blessed," which seems soon lost in the din of wicked, sinners and scoffers, the psalm comes to vibrant signs of life and choice, the profound, gritty, determined, choice to root by and in the river. And like parched pilgrims in this darkened wasteland that threatens to consume us, we find at the epicentre of the psalm—literally the word that stands at the linguistic centre with as many words before as after—the reality of vibrant fruit and all the promise of future life it entails. We love how Tim has carefully captured with color and flourish the "fruit" that is the psalm's heart.

There is something stunningly defiant in the essential character of all fruit. It is borne to hold the seeds of new life. To be scattered all about, as in Tim's rendering. Its purpose is to stretch forward, beyond even its own death, to a new life, to wrench a new generation from the decaying present. Here, in this metaphor of the fruitful tree, nourished by a river that gives life and flows in spite of—and perhaps even, for a time, because of—the surrounding misery, lies the precious promise of this threshold psalm. For us all, we have this choice: Where will I root, what fruit will I bear? It would be so lovely if the tree stood by the river and bore its happy fruit amidst the smiling sunshine of a breezy day as fluffy clouds scudded across the friendly sky. Instead, to bear fruit "in season" is to wait for that season to come. For the leaf to "not wither," it must endure withering forces—or how can it "not wither"? How can there be prospering if there is no pressing on, in spite of the overwhelming rationale to despair of the encroaching darkness? This is a defiant, rooted, persistent, obedient, radically hopeful tree that, amidst all the abundant rationale to shrink back, chooses to bear fruit! This is what I choose to wake into every day, even as so many of my days are now past. This persistence drives me to ask Chris so often, what can I write now? Once resolved to live, how can I still bear fruit for the One who has so rooted me in His grace?

Here in this welcoming psalm is our daily choice, to choose to live a fruitful life, today, in this moment, amidst all the surrounding discordance. Hope is surely not a method, but it is a choice. There is no more profound choice for each day than to root deeper, draw more nourishment still from the streams of living water by which we have chosen to be planted. Thus rooted, defying all the encroaching and angry darkness, with every quaking breath we can summon, with all the saints who have for generations pondered these words, we declare for ourselves, I am "Blessed" and so, by Grace, bear much fruit, for His glory.

My prayer, as you find your own encouragement in this psalm is to look forward, beyond the profound and sometimes deep disappointment of today, into a season of fruit-bearing. For that, we must each find a "new song" to sing unto the Lord and to the singing of those new songs, we shall now turn.

With my blessing that you each be "Blessed!"

Jim

Letter #30

June 9, 2022

Dear friends,

In a recent conversation with my son Chris, I told him it was time for us to write about singing a "a new song." Since he is no longer quite so predisposed to simply take what I say at face value, he probed my suggestion with "why?" and "why now?" Pressing his point, he asked, "Dad, why is it so important that we now sing a new song? More to the point, why do *you* want to sing a 'new song'?" And so I explained to him that for generations, even millennia, pandemic periods of history have been followed by periods of great creative flourishing, often made possible by the disruption of the pandemic. The grain trade in Old Testament times brought plague, about which the psalmist writes in Psalm 91. The deep discouragement of Psalm 88 is followed by the affirmation of Psalm 91, and then the whole psalter lifts its head through the psalms of ascent and the final doxology. The Renaissance followed the egalitarian destruction of the European plague. The Spanish Flu gave rise to massive changes in public health. A local grocer reports a kinder and gentler and less frenetic public as the Covid restrictions have eased. So, I told Chris, we need to write about "a new song" because I am excited to see what flourishing will follow this darkness that we have all known.

In many ways, the pandemic has exposed each of us to a deeper darkness than we are accustomed to know. We each know something about depression. For some, it is a deep and abiding and frightening darkness that seems at times to crush our spirits and silence our capacity to even desire, let alone realize, anything else. For others, and I know this reality better for myself, a brooding malaise hangs over days and sometimes weeks. Here in our hospital, some of my new "neighbours" have found their lives so darkened by the actions of others that they seem no longer able to be honest with themselves in their despair, let alone with the rest of us. I know for myself that there is a habit to such acedia against which I must guard my own spirit. Furthermore, as I reflect on my own life, some most creative periods have arisen from deep discouragement. And so now, in this post-pandemic confusion in which we all live, with war and inflation dominating our public discourse, I choose to sing a new song. Psalm 33 gives words to my cry…

> Sing joyfully to the Lord, you righteous;
> it is fitting for the upright to praise him.
> Praise the Lord with the harp;
> make music to him on the ten-stringed lyre.
> Sing to him a new song;
> play skillfully, and shout for joy.
>
> For the word of the Lord is right and true;
> he is faithful in all he does.
> The Lord loves righteousness and justice;
> the earth is full of his unfailing love. …
>
> We wait in hope for the Lord;
> he is our help and our shield.
> In him our hearts rejoice,
> for we trust in his holy name.
> May your unfailing love be with us, Lord,
> even as we put our hope in you.

Like the fresh manna that the Lord provided to His people as they navigated the wilderness, so it is to sing a new song. As the manna was collected each day, so we sing a new song each day. After the darkness we expect a new flourishing. Along with my favourite hymn writer Isaac Watts (1674-1748)…

> I sing the mighty power of God that made the mountains rise
> That spread the flowing seas abroad and built the lofty skies.
> I sing the wisdom that ordained the sun to rule the day;
> The moon that shines bright at his command, and all the stars

obey.

There is not a plant or flower below but makes your glories known;
And clouds arise, tempests blow, by order from your throne.
While all that borrows life from you is ever in your care,
And everywhere that I may be, God you are present there.[19]

And so my prayer for each of us is...

Dear Lord, as Elijah was looking up to heaven, he was uplifted by a chariot of fire, so may I always keep looking up towards heaven. Even when my eyes are cast down, protect me from slipping into the dark mire of depression by putting a new song in my heart, giving me even the desire and strength to sing. Lord, let me so trust you that I sing that new song, that I anticipate your goodness, that I expect your enjoyment of even me and so, bring me joy that can spill out for others, even when they are cast down and their eyes are not lifted up. Amen

In friendship,

Jim

Letter #31

June 16, 2022

Dear friends,

As I have been reflecting with expectancy upon what new vibrancy might emerge from this global pandemic, I return again and again to a sense that it is in our emotions that a renaissance of sorts will likely unfold. We have tested the boundaries of our capacity for rational thought, and while industrial prowess remains remarkable, the unravelling we are all experiencing as human beings seems beyond our mere cognitive capacities. Our spirits have been literally pounded by isolation, by anxiety for loved ones, by institutional instability, by a dizzying array of emergent dis-order, all weighing on a deep angst that our ancient faith is somehow outdated and irrelevant. In the whipsawing of emotions that inevitably follows this kind of global crisis—one moment the hope of recovery, another the imminence of further collapse—we find our emotional muscles getting a workout that has them on fire. Yet here, in this place of emotional dislocation, we are invited—indeed we need—to sing a new song. The landscape that shapes our emotional "dustbowl" might not change, but we can choose to view that same landscape quite differently.

When the prayer book was in its original compilation, it was not without good reason that a foundational building block of morning prayer was what we now know of as the "Venite," based largely on Psalm 95. For the psalmist, a lot has happened since he expressed his "new song" in Psalm 33. We have entered the depth of his sin with Bathsheba, reflected in Psalm 51, and most recently lived through the "deadly pestilence" of Psalm 91. Here, with Psalm 95 we have begun a long ascent that culminates in the doxology psalms at the end of the psalter. So, in the order of morning prayer, we are led through the confession and into this healing of our emotional wounds out of which we "sing for joy"! Out of David's deep self-inflicted wounding and depression, broken and in profound despair over his own emotional bankruptcy, he invites us to "come before (the Lord) with thanksgiving." This is the gritty stuff of emotional healing and renewal. This is where many of us are today. This is our moment to choose. Please join with me…

Come, let us sing for joy to the Lord;
let us shout aloud to the Rock of our salvation.
Let us come before him with thanksgiving
and extol him with music and song.

For the Lord is the great God,
the great King above all gods.
In his hand are the depths of the earth,
and the mountain peaks belong to him.
The sea is his, for he made it,
and his hands formed the dry land.

Come, let us bow down in worship,
let us kneel before the Lord our Maker;
for he is our God
and we are the people of his pasture,
the flock under his care.

Psalm 96 continues this theme with…

Sing to the Lord a new song;
sing to the Lord, all the earth.
Sing to the Lord, praise his name;
proclaim his salvation day after day.
Declare his glory among the nations,
his marvelous deeds among all peoples.

Most of the time, especially now, we do not so much feel like we *want* to sing a new song as *need* to. As so much of what we have all known as western Christianity trembles before the relentless onslaught of secularism, we need to choose to live as expectant peoples. The Lord gave us the psalter not that our minds would be enriched so much as so that our emotions might be healed; so that we could pray not only the simple words of our Lord's prayer, but also cry the anguish of the psalmist. My children have said of me that I do not so much live in the past loss of my own story as in the future discovery of God's story. That is certainly my preference. The emotional habit that helps is to choose, this day, now, in the midst of whatever discourages, to sing a new song.

My prayer for each of you, my friends, is that you find such a song for today and that you grow expectant that you will again find one for tomorrow.

In friendship,

Jim

Letter #32

June 23, 2022

Dear friends,

Every time I hear the Psalmist express his discovery of being possessed by a "new song of joy," I feel again like the clay in the potter's hands, being still remoulded, yearning that the Potter would eventually be satisfied with the re-shaping of my life. I thought I was ready for glory when I came here to this small private nursing hospital and hospice seven months ago. My children were clearly sceptical that I was ready for glory. Now I know they were right! My favourite prophet as a teenager was the tender-hearted Jeremiah, who visited his own "potter's shed" to see God shaping and re-shaping his life through many afflictions, past, present, and future. I now see that as long as we are self-made products, we are not nearly ready to enter glory.

We need to be "de-selfed" by being re-shaped again "in the image and likeness of Christ," by asceticism. My favourite exemplar is St. Anthony (c. 296-373), father of the Coptic Church in Egypt. Born into a wealthy family, he gave away all his riches to the poor and the hungry. He traveled around within sight of Mount Sinai, where Moses had heard God give him the ten commandments, and now where Anthony was seeking to be saturated by the Holy Scriptures, able to memorize all the Psalter. His dwelling place was a cave, overlooking the south-west corner of the Red Sea.

Before Anthony could settle down to his new cave home, he had to clear his dwelling place that was full of snakes. That "metaphorized" all the temptations that can possess us, once we start to live the ascetic life, endeavouring to become aesthetic, "beautiful in the grace of God." Then, for Anthony, the rage of Satan began, sending an army of devils to attack him in every possible way. Like Adam and Eve placed in a garden of paradise, Anthony thought his cave would also be paradisal, only to find an army of devils sorely wounding him. His only defence was to recite the words of the Psalmist, which he repeats some six times over, especially when attacked by demons (Ps. 27:3; Ps. 118:7), and being faced by the apparition of Satan (Ps. 68:1-3). Then wondrously, by reciting such Psalms, the demons and even the Devil fled, totally defeated.

It was through this great adversity that Anthony was given such vigilance that God would reveal to him in dreams. On one occasion, two travellers in the desert came to see him, one already dead from lack of water, the other dying, without water. So he sent an assistant with water, to save his life. Hospitality became Anthony's alter ego. So why then did he live a solitary life? His response was: "Because, as fish need water, monks need solitude to absorb love," as the apostle Paul does, in the epistle to the Romans, chapter 8. Like the apostle Luke, Anthony was a physician of the emotions, all needing to be healed.

Out of this solitary hardship, Anthony became world-famous. As Augustine of Hippo remarked in his *Confessions*, these—i.e. Desert Fathers—"have not had our [Classical] schooling, yet they stand up and storm the gates of heaven."[20] The Emperor Constantine and his son often wrote to Anthony, seeking his wise counsel, but like the apostle Paul, St. Anthony could reply: "yet not I, but the grace of God that was with me" (1 Cor. 15:10).

No wonder Athanasius, the reporter on Anthony's life and sayings, could stand up to an army of Arians in Cairo, as St. Anthony had stood up to Satan and his devils.

So many hymns we could use, to communicate the asceticism of St. Anthony. But one of my favourites is Charles Wesley's dedication to the Lord:

> O thou who camest from above
> the pure celestial fire to impart,
> Kindle a flame of sacred love
> on the mean altar of my heart!
>
> There let it for thy glory burn

with inextinguishable blaze,
and trembling to its source return,
in humble prayer and fervent praise.

Jesus, confirm my heart's desire
to work, and speak, and think for Thee;
Still let me guard the holy fire,
and still stir up thy gift in me;

Ready for all Thy perfect will,
my acts of faith and love repeat,
till death Thy endless mercies seal,
and make the sacrifice complete.[21]

My prayer for each of us is simple...

Lord, help us to live like the life of Anthony, clothed like a child, learning to live the gospel story, and warmed by the ardour of the psalms of David, to beautify your name. Amen.

In friendship,

Jim

Letter #33

Editor's Note: This letter, like the few that may follow—though we are never sure where these journeys will take us—derives from notes and some conversations over the past few weeks, on the subject of "salvation." As always, your scribe seeks to faithfully report, like the embedded journalist, from the frontier of the ever-roving mind of our Dad and your friend. Restless, immensely curious, thematically persistent, Dad declares himself to be a very joyful man. To closely follow his trail, however, requires both intellectual and interpretive agility that taxes lesser mortals who occasionally miss publication deadlines. The tardy arrival of this week's missive is a function of conflicting priorities in the editorial department and not, he would most earnestly have you know, any suggestion that our most blessed 99-year-old should be lagging in vigor!

July 1, 2022

Dear friends,

In the weekend of celebration of Canada Day in the north and Independence Day in the south, all of North America is somehow in celebration of "freedom" and the declared identity of country and flag and all that those symbols are fashioned to represent in our collective imaginations. The very word "freedom" leads us to focus on that from which freedom has been granted, and perhaps achieved, though many sceptics have plenty of grounds for rightful questions. Indeed, the "culture wars" of the US, the recent "celebrations" in Hong Kong, war in Europe, inflation fears, market crashes, recessionary threats, post- (or is it inter-?) pandemic woes might all make us wonder just how much "freedom" is actually being realized, even in the "free" world. Sensibly, perhaps, the celebrations this year somehow seem more tepid, more aspirational than realized, more obligatory than existential.

For many of us, for most of our lives in the journey of faith, we have viewed and experienced our "salvation" through a judicial lens. That, through Christ, the law has been satisfied and that we are thus deemed not guilty. Indeed, the law only has two possible states for the accused: guilty or not-guilty. I'm reminded of the cup of water that can only be either empty or not-empty. Or the Hippocratic mantra of western medicine that there can be harm or "no harm." Even the mighty Google figured out a few years ago that their aspiration of "Don't be evil" was woefully inadequate and that perhaps doing some good was required! But as Christians, we tend still to get stuck in this sense that we have been "saved from" and forget to move on and realize that we have also been "saved to." I have learned myself of late that it is not enough for me to have no medical reason to die, and so be "saved" from the death I thought was both imminent and welcome, but I also have to fully embrace being alive. To be "not dead" only gets me half-way. To be "not-guilty" does not make me free. To be "not empty" does not mean my cup runneth over. If we see our salvation only in judicial terms, we are still only half alive, at best, simply not-dead!

As we view our many interactions with Covid, we are finding that there are a growing number of people who though no longer sick, are hardly well. Long-Covid is not just a disease of our bodies. Many of us are suffering from a spiritual long-Covid that permanently locks us in a wearying place, where our salvation has set us free from guilt, but our emotions remain permanently scarred and impeded in their motions, such that we are not fully alive. My dear Rita long suffered from a physical restriction in her joints from arthritis. She could still move, but hardly with fluid motion and without pain. I wonder how many of us find our emotional joints equally scarred and stiffened to the point of immobility. The law pronounces us "not guilty," yet it cannot infuse us with life.

Just recently, I was stunned to discover that a medical procedure I was certain my body had required was just an illusion of my mind. It took my doctor, showing me that I had no requisite scar, before I would believe that I was indeed mistaken in my own diagnosis of my presumed ailment. So sure was I of my condition that I experienced symptoms that I later learned were simply not possible. This is the gift for us of the psalmist who, like my kind physician, helps us to see that where we thought we were wounded, and have lived out of that wounding perhaps for decades, we are far from merely "not-dead," but that our emotions can be made alive and our beings full of health.

In the next few weeks, this is the path I hope we can explore together, to embrace a salvation that heals our emotions to Life and to its abundance. The Great Physician comes to us through the psalms and through the voices of the ancients who knew no limits of mere judicial salvation, such that Christ heals our emotions and enables us to embrace a being alive that is so far beyond "not-guilty" that it is real freedom. Today, may you each see that "quickening ray" that promises that soon, the emotional dungeons in which we so often imprison ourselves, can be filled with light, and with chains fallen off we can each, with the hymnist, walk into real freedom.

In friendship,

Jim

Letter #34

July 7, 2022

Dear friends,

In all the changing scenes of life, we all get new perspectives. I continue to find this the case not only through the window and across the beaches of Kitsilano to the north-shore mountains, where I live, but as the "dark glass" through which I have always "barely seen" grows clearer as I near my Father's eternal presence. It is strange now for me to communicate with many of you whom I once knew as students and who are now retired from the professions for which you trained over so many years, including at Regent. Change of setting brings change of perspective.

As a child, I was never that enthused about being with my father when he was displeased with me. What child enjoys a critical parent? Yet, when his attitude changed, I found that it was a joy to be with him. If, as the Shorter Catechism reminds us, our "chief aim is to glorify God and enjoy Him forever," how might that be possible if we insist on any sense that we are forever scolded by our Heavenly Father in His displeasure with us? As I reflected in my last letter, we need to experience in God something far deeper than simply being declared "not guilty" lest we live in the fear that His verdict might at any time change. Fear is what fills the vacuum of love in our hearts. Fear lies at the heart of most of our unhealthy emotions. Our worship to our heavenly Father is simply living in His eternal presence, recipients of His Eternal Love. Then we truly can worship Him, gloriously free from wrong emotions, all basically originating from fear.

As I reflect upon "Jesus"—meaning the Lord, our Saviour—I do so as He is the Eternal Physician, who heals me of all my perverse emotions that keep me from not being always the recipient of His Eternal Love. From this new perspective that like the psalmist "puts a new song in my heart" (Ps. 40:3), we then find that all the early Church

Fathers saw "sin" not in a legal category, but in a medical category. The Apostle Luke, being himself a medical doctor, particularly narrates the miracles of healing Jesus performed, as well as the "Psychiatric Doctor," facing angry, jealous, callous, and other emotionally handicapped individuals, whether leaders of the Jews like the Scribes or Pharisees, or the members of the crowds.

All the early Fathers, from the 2nd century until the later centuries, unanimously identified "sin" and its need of healing in medical and therapeutic terms. George Herbert, the great poetic reformer of the 17th century, continued this tradition and still maintained his therapeutic view of our salvation as the "healing of our emotions." Herbert viewed himself as a "pastor" or shepherd of his flock and stood at the porch to welcome them to the Sunday morning service. His didactic and, for some, difficult poem, "The Church Porch," also carries the title "Perirrhanterium," which in Ancient Greek referred to the sprinkler of holy water. Herbert invites us to prepare to come to worship through a welcome that is cleansing of harmful emotions to be "cleansed in the holy water, from apathy, alcoholism, inattention, swearing, the terrible emotion of pride, insincerity, inconsistency, greed, extravagance, curiosity, bad-tempered, quarrelsome, cynically mirthful, vanity, envy, extravagance, depression, meanness, that is all negative emotions that would make one incapable of being a worshipper of God in all His Holiness."[22]

He affirms that we are in God's house by God's permission, concluding with the admonition; "Resort to sermons, but to prayers most: Prayer is the end of preaching."

To enter the place of worship through the "Church Porch" is not to enter for the sake of some intellectual exercise, but to be cleansed of harmful emotion and to be nearer to God's holy presence, cleansed and healed emotionally, to be always in prayer worshipping in the beauty of holiness. It was only later, with Calvin who trained as a lawyer, that the doctrine of salvation became a legal category and the therapeutic cleansing for real health was lost. Sin became disobedience rather than the full sweep of our emotional harming from which we so deeply need to be healed so that we can be fully alive.

As we each reflect on how we have narrowed Christ's welcome to us through mere legal justification, my prayer for us each is that we might enter His Presence as through the Church Porch, to be welcomed with a cleansing sprinkling, a cleansing of our emotional selves so as to enter so much more fully into His presence and the abundance of a full Life that He alone can provide and for which we are saved. Not just saved from death, but saved to Life!

Help us, dear Saviour of our Souls, to become aware we are "sinning all through our life," when we are never healed of fear, blocking out Your Eternal Love! So, help us Lord, to rest in Your Eternal Love, as the complete environment of our souls, blessed by Your promise that "perfect love drives out fear" (1 John 4:18). Amen.

In friendship,

Jim

Letter #35

July 7, 2022

Dear friends,

As we continue to explore the loving healing of our tender God in the unreached dimension of our emotions, I want to begin with what seems on the face of it to be a radical and to our 21st century ears, even jarring. Asaph, the psalmist, writes in Psalm 82:6, "I said, "you are 'gods'; you are all sons [and daughters!] of the Most High."" Most of us struggle with our emotional lives, with anxiety or with the kind of fearfulness I knew so well as a young man, or that numbing we choose so as to avoid what hurts too much to engage. Some whom I know and love experience those deeper and darker places, places of depression, and yet, the psalmist challenges this low sense of self with a virtual absurdity. For the ancients, the "gods" were transcendent, lived beyond the realm of the ordinary and seemed just like our envied neighbour to "have it all together," to be "successful," to have such "confidence" or "capability." The "gods" were who I wasn't but wished I was. They were the epitome of what was beyond my own reach, for myself. And yet, in the previous verse of Psalm 82, Asaph writes, "The 'gods' know nothing, they understand nothing. They walk about in darkness." It seems the emotionally self-possessed "glitterati" don't glitter after all!

For the Desert Fathers, the most prevalent emotional sickness was acedia (accidie, in Latin). Anthony likened it to "a large river of sadness whose delta had many rivulets, such as sloth, or boredom, disgust and languor, lassitude and torpor, all in a vague dissatisfaction with the status quo that poured its great river into the ocean of our emotions."[23] Others called it the "noonday devil" because for the ascetic monks, sitting in the cave in the heat of the day, were then most tested, reflecting—in our more modern vernacular—"Being here seemed like a good idea at the time, but now I'm not so sure"! (I can just hear my dear Rita with her sensible suggestions that she'd be depressed sitting in a cave all day just meditating!). St. Anthony had good reasons to question why he might have traded wealth for poverty, food for hunger, servants for hard and demanding work. These were the times when he was tested most deeply.

Such times of testing can so easily lead us to a kind of mindless fatalism reflected in the well-known lyrics "Que sera, sera...whatever will be, will be."[24] No, we are not victims. We are not passive creatures stuck with whatever grieves our spirits. Our emotional struggles are very real, but they are not supreme. While it took me decades to learn that my own fearfulness was not a life sentence, it was moving through that fear, not remaining stuck there, that saw me through. Another of the ancients of our faith, Gregory of Nyssa, reminds us that to be made in the image and likeness of God is to possess the former by gift but the latter by will. The gift is the potential of Imago, but we choose our likeness with minds that are equipped to seek healing, perhaps—and even often—through the therapeutic skills of others, for whom we may simply just need to choose to show up and receive their help.

As the flood tides of this pandemic seem to be receding, at least for the moment, they reveal the immense darkness and damage of mental illness that has gripped so many of us and our loved ones. Many of us and our friends sit each day with St. Anthony, in the heat of the noonday sun, our spirits scorched with the searing heat of so much separation and anger and division and dis-ease. It is hard sometimes to even want to move out of this deep sadness that smothers too much. But that is not who we are. It is not our "lot" to be less than the "gods," the cheer-filled folks who struggle not. We are more than the imagined "fortunate few" whose emotional well-being seems to us, in our struggles, to be all tidied up and in order...we are all "sons [and daughters!] of the Most High" (Ps. 82:6). Image-bearers!—who can choose to embrace the likeness of our Heavenly Father.

My prayer for you is that you not become caught in what is, or seems to be, inevitable, or that to which you feel confined or trapped emotionally, but that you catch a glimpse of the glorious potential you have in Christ to take on His likeness, to flourish in being Image bearers. The trap of acedia can smother us all. Join with me as I press on, toward the goal, to win the prize for which God has called me—as He has called you each—heavenward in Christ Jesus (Phil. 3:14).

In friendship,

Jim

(For some reading in this area see: Dr. Jean-Claude Larchet, *Therapy of Spiritual Illness, Vol. One,* (Montreal, QC: Alexander Press, 2017) 16-17, 20-21.

Letter #36

July 17, 2022

Dear friends,

In this past week, I have been exploring more deeply what it means, for me, to know the healing of the Lord in the realm of my emotions. So much of my academic life has been grounded on what I think and can "fathom" intellectually, yet as those faculties continue to wane, I find I must more deeply cry the prayer of Augustine, "Let me know you, Lord, who know me; let me know you even as I am known," and that leads me to allow the healing grace of God to reach deeper into my own emotional life than I have allowed before.[25] These past days I have been wrestling with the dimensions of pride and humility that shape the ground of so much of what we experience emotionally. In the journey out of pride and into humility we are carrying a "payload," as it were, of our identity and our sense of whether we need to protect and enhance that identity, or whether it is held by an Other. As I came face to face with the choices of others that have gone before, I felt a deep conviction that I had still so much to learn. So exhausting was this encounter with the revealing humility of others that I slept for an entire day afterwards.

As we explore the health of an emotion and invite the Lord to grant us insight as to our own soul health or sickness in that regard, we find that it is by examining antithesis that we can learn much. Certainly, this is true of pride and humility for humility is, by its very nature, opposed to both vainglory and pride. I think you will find that your most real and trusted friends are the humble. For the humble are never in rivalry with others, while the proud always are. That is why the proud are always isolated, not knowing others, nor themselves. So, the proudly impetuous disciple, Peter, not knowing himself, could not really know who Jesus was. In a strange way, he was honest in saying to the servant girl in Herod's palace, he did not "know" Jesus, asserting this three times, as a way of bluntly and flatly contradicting her assertion. Later, Jesus asked Peter three times, "Do you love me?" Peter had to learn painfully what he later wrote that yes indeed, "God... shows favor to the humble" (1 Pet. 5:5).

The Psalmist David, having committed three terrible sins—sexually with Bathsheba; as a murderer of her husband by putting him as commander of his army on the front of the battle, where he was slain; and worst of all, in having a census made of his armed force, which was forbidden by God, as showing a lack of trust in God's Word that He would always defend Israel—then becomes repentant, now declares early in his lists of lamentations, that God "forgets not the cry of the humble" (Ps. 9:12). For now, David had experienced human intimacy with God, as a humbled man. Now, David no longer experienced the distance and separation produced by pride, which had generated sin, which Adam and Eve had cosmologically caused— "The Fall of Man." Two more recent examples have moved my heart such that I want to share them with you for your encouragement.

In early 17th century England, after the confusion of the Civil War, George Herbert (1593-1633) set out to be a reforming pastor. We saw last week how he welcomed his parishioners to the porch of the church with a holy sprinkling. His parish was not in a grand place, and he eschewed fame. He did not even publish his outstanding poetry. This was done after his death by his friend Nicolas Ferrar—who suggests, concerning Herbert's humility, that Herbert was quite indifferent to his professional status, preferring to be a "country parson," a choice that cost him more stately appointments. He even once set out to take on a church that was in ruins and in dire need of repair. Indifferent to the qualifications Cambridge University required for ordination, he took his time in getting any qualification. Today, no doubt, he would be horrified that any should be called "a Master of Divinity," marvelling instead at how little of the mysteries of God could be fathomed much less mastered! Ferrar notes that "next [to] God, [Herbert] loved that which God himself has magnified above all things, that is, his Word."[26] This contributed to his own cultivated brilliance of language, whether in speech or in poetry.

Thus Herbert stood apart, with no interest whatever about preferment or advancement, for his passion for God's word, his devotion to serve God's people, and by embodying the essentials of Christian living together, by the daily practice of praying with his wife and three nieces (daughters of his deceased sister) twice a day. In his poems he has only six that focus on humility. In the first, he sees that as congregants enter the church, its floor has a mosaic with the word "Humility" designed on it. He shows the humility of Mary Magdalene as a repentant prostitute wiping the feet of Jesus, "with pensive humbleness would live and tread."[27] Finally, he directs the congregants' attention to the humility of the Son of God, "for what Christ in humbleness began, We, Him in glory call, the Son of Man." At this stage of my life, I find myself deeply challenged by Herbert to reflect on a pattern in his life that I have too often resisted as a marker for my own. I am humbled by his example.

A second exemplar is Martin Luther, reformer of the 17th century. In great irony, we depict him as a giant figure of a man, defying the Roman Catholic emissaries at the Diet of Worms in 1521. "Here I stand, I can do no other," we famously hear him say. Some see him as the "icon of the individual," as Ronald Rittgers observes.[28] Ironically, Luther is the exact opposite. Rather he is, like George Herbert, one of the humblest of men. For Luther scarcely saw he had "a self" at all. In Luther's early years of ministry, he had learnt and taught the Psalms, seeing how David abases himself as a repentant sinner. He learned that the goal of human existence is to come to non-existence like Adam now is, and be renewed as Christ has been resurrected, to be now no longer "in self" but "in Christ." His identity is no longer "in Luther." In his lectures on the Epistle to the Romans (1515-16), he states, "The purpose of this letter, is to humiliate the proud, and teach them they need grace, by which to live."[29] As Rittgers notes, this is still so shocking to scholars today that there is still enormous controversy about the role of humility in our salvation. All this arose from Luther's view of God as depicted in the psalms. Humility, for Luther, is not a word that can be defined in a dictionary but can only be witnessed in the saints of God, like George Herbert and Martin Luther.

I have been deeply challenged by my brief reflections on these two men and how they allowed the Lord to shape in their emotional life, a deep humility of spirit. And so, as my friends, I pray for you…

Dear Lord, we are beginning to realize that it is only in the communion of saints, where saints like George Herbert and Martin Luther abide eternally with Thee, that we can voice with the words of Martin Luther, that it is not "I" that lives any longer, but that it is in the new identity of "Christ in me" that we have our identities. Forgive us, Lord, for putting so much distorted emphasis on "My ministry" or "I am me." Amen.

In friendship,

Jim

Letter #37

July 21, 2022

Dear friends,

As I have been reflecting in these past weeks on both our need for and the mechanisms of the Lord's healing of our emotions, I am drawn to a reality that has shaped my own life profoundly: the emotion of fear or, as I have often voiced inwardly, of timidity. Recently, I was reading in the fourteenth chapter of Proverbs to help me reflect and then write further concerning fear and its corollaries. I am beginning to see how, in this chapter, we see many dimensions of fear being explored: fear of the Lord, fear of others, and fear for the future, to name but a few.

Again and again in this text, the writer upholds a desirable fear of the Lord. In verse 2, "Whoever fears the Lord walks uprightly, but those who despise Him are devious in all their ways." As we know well from our own experiences, devious people are like snakes slithering around us. We do not know when they are going to try to poison our relations with other people. They are like the serpent in the Garden of Eden that caused the cosmic Fall of Mankind, in distrust and fear, and indeed, leading to madness. Those who "trust themselves" are so blinded that no one can trust them!

As a youth, I thought the Bible was a boring book. We heard it read, or read it on Sunday, totally unaware that the whole of Creation originated in and is sustained by the Word of God. This verse is telling us that people who despise God are as mad as the Mad Hatter in Alice in Wonderland, or as Shakespeare's Falstaff. Alas, we are so surrounded by such madness in this age of secularism that I find myself irritated with the crowds around me, for whom "there is no fear of God before their eyes" (Rom. 3:18). Certainly, most of us live around "normal, nice, kind people." Yes, we do, because all mankind were created in God's image and likeness. But when sin entered into the world, we all became mad, without God's Holy Spirit renewing our minds, to become wise.

We can only "walk upright" when we do so with integrity, yet also in being right-minded, and right-related with God and Man; and we are cautioned to, "stay away from a fool, for you will not find knowledge on their lips" (Prov. 14:7).

There are other affirmations to Fear the Lord. In verse 16, I read "The wise fear the Lord and shun evil, but a fool is hotheaded and yet feels secure." And again, in verse 26, "Whoever fears the Lord has a secure fortress, and for their children it will be a refuge." While these two verses affirm a fear of the Lord, they also hint at two other fears that beset us. Why does the hot-headed fool feel secure, I wonder? Here is the one whose affirmation comes from what others think, from the feedback of others, from the affirmation from others, from a sense of belonging that is earned through reinforcement of (foolish) behavior by others. Just recently, in a conversation with one of my daughters, I was exploring with her how I have been shaped by my attention to what others thought, of wanting to be associated with those of stature, even to prize scholarship and its credentials for their own sake. So many of us experience some sense of "imposter syndrome," alleviated only by the approbation we receive from others. This first text challenges this foundation of our identity, as if to say to us, "Do not fear the opinions of others who might exclude you from their foolish company, but instead, fear the Lord. Hold Him in highest esteem!"

The second verse sets up another contrast for us: fear of the Lord, and fear for the security of our children. There was a time, earlier in my life, when culturally and economically everything seemed to be opening and expanding and growing. There were wars and rumours of war to be sure, but the post-war period seemed expansive and hopeful. Our own journey as a family to Canada opened huge opportunities for our children through which we have each been immeasurably blessed. But that has shifted, and I sense the fear for future generations in the life of our children and our grandchildren, whether from the macro forces of climate change, secularization or culture wars, or the more micro forces of relationship fragmentation, economic pressures or the creaking angst from grinding pandemic. This verse challenges my anxiety for my children, their children and now their children. Rather, to fear the Lord is to enter a fortress that will be a refuge for my family. How can it be that at 99, with limited ability to walk, bounded by a lovely but small room in a hospital, I can shelter my family in a "fortress" where they are "secure"? This is surely a strange wisdom!

Our Proverbs text continues for me with "The fear of the Lord is a fountain of life, turning a person from the snares of death" (v 27). A moral reasoning is that God himself supplies "the water of life," so that we have Jesus's promise as He gave to the Samaritan Woman at the Well, "whoever drinks the water I give them will never thirst" (John 4:14). Then, the "snares of death" are the unbelieving thoughts of doubts about God and of His existence, which certainly cause death. As I find my body aging, I see how clearly "death" can occur long before the heart stops beating or the brain waves are stilled. We can each face a death of hope, locked in a cell of fear, not of the Lord, but fear of others and their opinions of us and paralyzed by a fearful future.

In some translations, Proverbs 14 is entitled "The Wise Woman." It is not without cause that the book of Proverbs concludes with an epilogue that praises the "wise wife," a woman that is wisdom. So much of what fear drives us to pursue is fleeting and of little significance in the end. As my son Chris has said to me, "I have spent an entire life fearful of so much that never happened!" The writer of Proverbs reminds us...

> Charm is deceptive, and beauty is fleeting;
> but a woman who fears the Lord is to be praised.
> Honour her for all that her hands have done,
> and let her works bring praise at the city gate.
> (Prov. 31:30)

So ends this remarkable book. It closes with a wise woman, wise in all her ways. In the Greek culture, Diana was the goddess of Greek culture. But to the God-fearing Hebrews, the epilogue of the book of Proverbs describes the Wife of Noble Character. She is the epitome of some ten blessings and virtues, both to her family and indeed to the whole community, extolled as she is by the rulers of the city. The pagan Corinthians might riot and stone the apostle Paul for defaming their goddess Diana, the goddess of Greek culture. But what is Greek culture when it is ignorant of God, the God, Creator of the whole Cosmos, and of everything that exists!

These reflections on the healing of our emotions and, for me, especially the emotion of fear, have been very helpful. They have been a turning point for me as I have grown to appreciate more the central virtue of seeking wisdom for my life. Yes, wisdom as human shrewdness for living in our workaday world, all of us need. But wisdom as the fear of the Lord is quite new in my life today. I am so grateful to the Lord for granting, in my very few remaining years, to have awareness of what is "the Wisdom of God." So, for you and for myself, I pray "Lord, may we all, as writer, editors, and readers, dwell more and more in the environment of being in the Fear of the Lord!"

In friendship,

Jim

Letter #38

August 4, 2022

Dear friends,

In my interactions with my son Chris, in the preparation of these letters, we have been exploring in our conversations together the ways in which the Lord seeks to heal our emotions. Chris, whose training and professional experience is quite different from my own, has been encouraging me to write much more from my own experience and lived reality and not just from the lived experience of others. As an academic, this has been challenging for me, yet I have been quite amenable to his encouragement. And so, today, I want to explore an emotion that is close to the fear that we explored last time—an emotion I have known all too well in my life—that of faintheartedness.

Faintheartedness is an expression of character, so deeply imbedded in our behaviour that it shapes and directs our other emotions. Like narcissism, or self-love, it is not subject to simple medical intervention. We can't just take a pill and be done with it. Yet we can be changed dramatically by our conversion to Christ, to become a new being "in Christ," and then, faintheartedness can literally melt away with our co-operation with the Holy Spirit.

In healthy families, there is competition among siblings to quietly compete with each other, the more siblings the better! I was the eldest of three, with two younger sisters. In my own timidity, I left the intense competition with my sister Ethel and moved to Oxford. My younger sister, Louie, sadly never really found her place—in contrast to her very accomplished elder sister. I have watched my own four children navigate their own birth order dynamics, each one expressing some faintheartedness in some way or another that they have, by God's grace, each found a way to overcome. I hope that in some way, I have encouraged each to find their own uniqueness and to celebrate that.

The early Fathers saw faintheartedness as a vice, indeed as a form of madness, certainly a sickness of the soul. John Cassian taught that "If the plague of vice infects the reasonable part, it will bring forth the vices of…faintheartedness."[30] As the apostle Paul assured Timothy, "For the Spirit God gave us does not make us timid, but gives us power, love and self-discipline" (2 Tim. 1:7). That is to affirm that God created us, as healthy human beings, to have confidence in God's help, in the Holy Spirit that Jesus in the Upper Room defined as "the Comforter" or *Paracletos.* It is an untranslatable word, because the "Paracletos" is the One who provides whatever need we have, in every circumstance of life. As a vice, faintheartedness was seen by the early church as really the work of the devil, to paralyze the conscience, allowing us to become vainglorious, thinking it is our right to be paid attention to, above all others. Then, we can become hypersensitive to anything negative we think others are doing, getting angry at the slightest negative thing. As a form of childishness, it is like the paralysis of a child that has never grown up. It is a terrible state of delusion.

So many have forgotten about Jesus speaking to all His disciples, then and now, about this amazing prayer, and in reciting the Lord's Prayer each day. Indeed, it is like giving up being a Christian at all, living in a daily dungeon of fear. In fact, it is the most tragic of all fears, forgetting all about God's love, which "casts out all fear." It is also a fear that leads to deception as we create stories to compensate for the truth that we fear will harm, rather than set us free.

In my own life journey, I can identify with the older lady that I used to see at our church, always at the back, always withdrawn from others, afraid to engage. Her much more engaged sister brought her each week, but she had not the capacity to will that for herself, lacking, it seemed to me, the courage and will to take initiative for herself without her sister as guide. As a young academic in Oxford, I knew this paralyzing fear for myself. I knew what it was to cross over the street so as not to encounter my more confident colleague as they marched along the pavement, oblivious to my crippling faintheartedness. I had not yet yielded to the extraordinary truth of Christ's promise that when we have faith in God, we can see mountains move! Not only are our emotions paralyzed, but our mind is also paralyzed, and our God-given imaginations for what is possible with Him are silenced. We see only in the black and white of fear. All the colour of possibility is drained away.

Most of you will have known me in a very different stage of my life. As I watched God's faithfulness through the early days of Regent, in securing our university affiliation in particular, my timidity was slowly changed to confidence, not in myself, but in the Living God. As I reflect back, I think three things were critical for me in this journey from "fear to faith." First, I chose to confront my deep-rooted anxiety by pursuing transparency and truth. Second, I was not alone and though I often felt like it, others walked beside me through it all. Third, I watched God do what only God can do and bring about changes in hearts and minds that I had no idea how to achieve. These formative events and years, though I was by then in what we might call "middle age," totally changed me. I became expectant that God would act in surprising and good ways. Sadly, I know many for whom the trap of faintheartedness has lasted much of a lifetime.

While there is much, too much, that would make our hearts faint, whether in the journeys of our families or in the wider events of our fragile world, our call as God's people is to walk alongside others and let them walk with us, to pray and build one another up, in love. My prayer for you is that where there are faint hearts, that they might be much encouraged as you risk all to expect God to do what lies beyond your imagination.

Fondly and in friendship,

Jim

Letter #39

August 11, 2022

Dear friends,

I have been mulling over our muddled relationship with the notion of "impassible." I suspect *[Note: as does your faithful scribe!]* that most of us do not spend much time pondering this word, but then at this stage, a lot of intriguing notions wander by in my days. As an adjective, if we use it, we think about blocked roads and missing bridges. When we think of it as a quality of a person, we tend to think of them as intransigent or perhaps obstreperous. Rarely would we consider it an attractive quality that we might rise into the day, leap to our feet, and declare with all the vigour appropriate to the new morning, "Today, I will be impassible!" Strangely, that is actually the problem. We should. Allow me to explain.

In these past weeks, we have been exploring the healing of our emotions, and soon we shall turn our attention to the role of Christ as Great Physician, as our Healer. For many of us, and I include myself, our wounded emotions are never healed because we keep them secure in a locked room that is designed to be perhaps our most impenetrable inner sanctum. Often, we do not even visit ourselves and have thrown away the key so many years ago that we cannot even find the door anymore. We have rendered whole parts of ourselves "impassible," an inner "no-go zone," usually guarded by a very powerful force that is generally fear-based. Yet, for the early Fathers, to be "impassible" was to have matured to a high ground, to have achieved humility and even conquered pride. This does not sound like our notion of being "impassible" at all. How could an attribute that keeps us locked away from others, and even from ourselves, be an evidence of maturity? On the face of it, this seems absurd!

Impassibility was the original health of Adam and Eve, like that of God's angels, as likewise His ministering spirits. Only "in Christ" can impassibility be made possible, to permit no false passion to affect the soul. Like a mirror that reflects clearly the presence of the one looking at it, so "Christian" impassibility can never distort nor remove. We human beings are all created "in the image and likeness of God." Before I go to sleep at night, I recite to myself the assuring words of the Psalmist: "I have calmed and quieted myself, I am like a weaned child with its mother" (Ps. 131:2)! Then I pray that in my dreams I might not have evil thoughts, but only have dreams where I sense there is the presence of God. So it often happens for me. For Christians, we can positively respond—when we are asked, "did you sleep well?"—"I slept like a baby, for Christ was present with me all night, with no nightmares, just glorious peace!" Then the following day, we can live with purity of mind; purity of thoughts that radiate love, joy and peace.

For many of you who knew my high-spirited Rita, you would know that I quite enjoyed teasing her. It just worked to make the day more interesting! I would ask her to respond to the adage: "Two men looked through prison bars. The one saw mud, the other stars. Which 'sight' did she want to have?" And her predictable response… "Of course, I want to see mud, because the other was hit on the back of the head and saw stars!" But with the aid of divine aseity—God's unique capacity to be only of Himself—we can all "sleep like a baby." For as we grow to embody the knowledge of God, and begin to respond to His eternal love, that divine aseity also begins to grow. All that we need is "contained within," for we have taken Christ into our beings and by His Spirit, He dwells in us. As the early Fathers experienced so clearly, living a given aseity then gives us freedom from this world, to live "heavenly-minded" in the true sense. It is the realm where Christ dwells and rules, and within this world we need nothing else. Our "impassibility" becomes not a protection of an unresolved hurt, but a protection against the broken world that lies outside and can only harm what is otherwise already healed. Becoming healed from false emotions is a zigzag climb, until we attain impassibility. This then makes it possible to love and be loved, no longer distracted and impeded by our lack of emotional health. So in the beautiful words of Kate B. Wilkinson (1859-1928), we sing and pray:

> May the mind of Christ my Saviour, live in me from day to day,
> by His love and power controlling all I do and say.
>
> May the Word of God dwell richly, in my heart from hour to hour,
> so that all may see I triumph, only through His power
>
> May the peace of God, my Father, rule my life in everything,
> that I may be calm to comfort sick and sorrowing.
>
> May the love of Jesus fill me, as the waters fill the sea,
> Him exalting, self-abasing, this is victory.
>
> May I run the race before me, strong and brave to face the foe,
> looking only unto Jesus, as I onward go.[31]

In friendship,

Jim

Letter #40

August 11, 2022

Dear friends,

There is something interminable about a mountain climb...until we reach the top. I think a lot about that, not that I am climbing mountains—though just getting out of bed some mornings feels a bit like it, I imagine—but I am keeping going. As we have been working through some exploration of what is means to be healed of our emotional suffering, I have been reflecting on this deep struggle that many of us experience, simply to keep on going. At my stage, it is easy to consider the milestone ahead as I reach for my 100th birthday, later this year in November. But what then? It's not that I find the challenge is physical—my doctors tell me that nothing is wrong medically, other than that I keep getting older—but how do I continue emotionally and imaginatively? Will I even have enough new ideas to write letters, when the replies so many of you have sent have so fueled my own imagination and filled my heart with deeper gratitude? Living, for many of us, is just hard work. Like an old car that has to occasionally stop, refuel, add air to tires and water to radiators, so each of us need new emotional energy if we are to express the love of God, as a resource for others. Over the years, and ever more so now, I have needed to find a way to be re-fueled with love for the journey.

As a younger man, when first I fell in love with my wife Rita, I was refreshed in the romance of our relationship. Even in her years of dementia, we found new ways to be refreshed in each other. In fact, as her capacity lessened, I found my love for her deepened, as I needed to hold her identity for her as her capacity to do so faded and diminished. It was a precious time in our lives together. Similarly, the Lord has found for me ways to be refreshed in His love for me as I learned to take the love of the ancient saints, in their love of the Lord, and let it inspire my own heart. The practical outworking of this very personal discovery was the introduction of Spiritual Theology as a discipline at Regent, inspired by the Franciscan universities in Spain and the spiritual journey of my own mother as a missionary in Spain, who especially loved St. Teresa of Avila. My mother had served, as a single woman, in the small pueblo of Piedralaves, only 20 miles away from Avila.

I marvel now at how the Lord drew from the roots of my own story an inspiration for keeping His love alive in me as an adult. As I began to teach the new courses on Spiritual Theology, I was drawn deeper into this realm and grew to find my own loves in the inspiring lives of these early saints. The Franciscan Catholics in colleges of Spain and Italy had already been inspired by a new revival of Franciscan Theology, from the sacramentalism of the Dominicans to a more personal theology. The Franciscans have throughout history been reformers, just as Pope Francis is today. So today, as I wake to yet another blessed day and wonder from where will come the desire and capacity to enter it fully, tired as my physical body may be, I find myself in this "first love" to which the Lord led me so many decades ago. Since we began these letters, the number of people asking to receive them has nearly tripled and I wonder, what shall I write now? When I ask my son and editor, Chris, that question, he just tells me to write what I am discovering today about the Lord and how He has inspired me today. But to respond to his simple challenge means I have to look, and I have to choose to look for inspiration. I cannot simply sit and wait for something to show up. I have to be looking, actively.

I find a rich source of daily inspiration in my favourite poets. Perhaps chief among my favourites is George Herbert, who in turn also inspired the poet Richard Crashaw. While Herbert loved the Lord gently, Crashaw loved Him with a passion, just as Theresa of Avila had done before. In Crashaw's eulogies to St. Teresa, he writes…

> O thou undaunted daughter of desires!
> By all thy dower of lights and fires;
> By all the eagle in thee, all the dove;
> By all thy lives and deaths of love;
> By all thy large draughts of intellectual day,

And by thy thirsts of love more large than they;
All thy brim-fill'd bowls of fierce desire,
By thy last morning's draught of liquid fire;
By the full kingdom of that final kiss
That seized thy parting soul, and seal'd thee His;
By all the Heaven thou hast in Him.[32]

It has been my gift to live for many years longer than my own mother who, in turn, outlived all expectations for her life. She and I have lived through very different eras, and yet we are both inspired by the zealous love of St. Teresa for her Lord. Such love fueled her life. Her inspiring example fuels my own. Knowing the days for me, the Lord has embedded in my own story, through the life of my own mother, the very food I would need to sustain me in my 99th year. This is the gift of Grace for which we must each seek and which we can all find. What we love, whom we love, defines who we are and whose we are. So, my prayer for you this day, in this season of your life, is that you might find revealed, perhaps in overlooked chapters of your own narrative, the seeds of Grace that now can yield a harvest of hope. I hope you can join with me to prayerfully sing with Laurie Klein,

I love you Lord, and I lift my voice,
to worship you, O my soul, rejoice!

Take joy my King, in what you hear,
may it be a sweet, sweet sound in your ear.[33]

In friendship,

Jim

Letter #41

August 25, 2022

Dear friends,

I suppose it is rather unremarkable that living as I do, in a hospital, I should be reminded rather often that there is a lot of sickness around and with that sickness, mercifully, a lot of care being given. Hardly surprising, anyone might reasonably think, but not very popular, and for most of my life, hospitals were a place I could not leave soon enough. They may well be filled with gracious care, but I hated them with a passion, perhaps because I had been so incarcerated in them as a young and rather sickly boy. Instead of being with my friends, I was sitting in an oxygen tent, wrestling with the misery of diphtheria. I'm not surprised that I grew to loathe the sight of a hospital. But that has all had to change, for now I not only visit but I live in one—and rather a nice one at that. So, it is unremarkable that I should be thinking and reflecting a lot on physicians and their ilk and, in particular, Christ as our healer.

In our hyper-individualistic culture, to be the solitary hero is esteemed. We herald "I did it my way." We prize individualism and self-sufficiency. We eschew dependence. Yet biblical language is never individualistic but "personal," as God Himself is One God in Three Persons. Becoming individualistic was the cause for "the Fall of Man." Humanity lost the identity God had given to us, and still expects us to have. This is a profound sickness that God still intends to heal, if we allow Him to be our great physician. The sickness of being alone is a "sickness" that no early Father, even by turning to the Old Testament prophets, could heal. Only Christ our Saviour-Healer can ever do that. Even the animals know their masters, even animals as stupid as a donkey, but Israel refused to know and relate to God as their Redeemer-Physician. It cost them dearly.

The foundations of our ancient European universities like Oxford, Paris, Strasbourg, Salamanca, and Rome, were monastic. Even today, in an echo of their distant past, these universities still provide that lecturers should both lecture and teach personally to each student also as a tutor, originally as having a "spiritual father." That is why we call the early Fathers of the churches "Spiritual Fathers." They were themselves following the counsel of the books of Proverbs and Ecclesiastes. Proverbs 11:14 reminds us that "for lack of guidance a nation falls, but victory (and by that I include our emotional healing) is found through many advisors." For all of us, to have no friend as a counsellor is a wretched state to be in, stripped bare, to bear no fruit to delight the lives of others. Only to have "the self" to guide one is blindness indeed. So the early Fathers were emphatic that to be wise is never to be self-taught. Such are deluded in false convictions. It is like wandering through an unmapped territory, refusing all guidance, just stumbling, lost, alone. Then as Ecclesiastes 4:10 warns us: "pity anyone who falls and has no one to help them up." Of course, we all need experienced guides who have travelled the same roads we are now on, who know the cul-de-sacs, the traps, snares, and dangers of wild animals, of which we are totally innocent. These metaphors of being lost, fallen down, covered with leaves, caught by traps, and encountering wild animals, are all graphic images that God originally stated in the creation of Adam, "It is not good to be alone."

I love the imagery of the prophet Isaiah in chapter 1:

> Why should you be beaten anymore?
> Why do you persist in rebellion?
> Your whole head is injured,
> your whole heart afflicted.
> From the sole of your foot to the top of your head
> there is no soundness—
> only wounds and welts
> and open sores,
> not cleansed or bandaged
> or soothed with olive oil.

(v. 5-6)

And the psalmist in Psalm 6…

> Lord, do not rebuke me in your anger or discipline me in your wrath.
> Have mercy on me, Lord, for I am faint; heal me, Lord, for my bones are in agony.
> My soul is in deep anguish. How long, Lord, how long?
>
> Turn, Lord, and deliver me; save me because of your unfailing love.
> Among the dead no one proclaims your name. Who praises you from the grave?
>
> I am worn out from my groaning.
>
> All night long I flood my bed with weeping and drench my couch with tears.
> My eyes grow weak with sorrow; they fail because of all my foes.
> (v. 1-7)

It takes an open and dependent heart to be healed by Grace. Michael Perry (1942-1996) captures well the cry of my own heart in his hymn.

> Heal me, hands of Jesus, and search out all my pain;
> restore my hope, remove my fear, and bring me peace again.
>
> Cleanse me, blood of Jesus, take bitterness away;
> let me forgive as one forgiven and bring me peace today.
>
> Know me, mind of Jesus, and show me all my sin;
> dispel the memories of guilt and bring me peace within.
>
> Fill me, joy of Jesus; anxiety shall cease,
> and heaven's serenity be mine, for Jesus brings me peace![34]

After a lifetime of never wanting to be around hospitals and their caring ways, I am now growing to appreciate that to eschew healing is to run from the very heart of a loving God. So many of us, in our often-desperate efforts to be self-sufficient, to fight against dependency, to insist on "my way," losing sight that in our creation, in our Image-bearing, we were never made to be alone. Look about and see, whom has the Lord placed to care for you and for whom has He placed you to care for others? For such is His way, each for the other. May it be so.

In friendship,

Jim

Section:

III

"The View from The Top"

Letters Written from ...
September, 2022 – November, 2022

Psalm #3 of Jim (September 2022 – November 2022)

1) Lord, my Lord, how excellent is Your name in all the earth!

2) You have filled my days with such abundance. There is morning and (after a short nap) there is evening. Day after blessed day. You have filled up my cup, and it overflows.

3) It seems there is so much to be done. So many books. So many letters. So many ideas! And to think, I thought all was done.

4) Father of mine, in heaven (hallowed be thy name), how I wonder that You should connect me around the world with such of Your servants in whom You have placed such trust. I see Your hand writ large in them all. You work Your mysterious ways, and yet include me in Your unfoldings.

5) I marvel at how You chose to draw me in, whether through Regent, or the Houston Centre, or in the works of others. How vital are Your ways. How blessed am I to still participate. It seems we are not done yet!

6) The birthday came and went. Thank You for that gathering, first of family then of friends. The cards were lovely, but I hope You didn't mind that I put them all away so soon. So much to do, time to move on, even a centenary… so quickly over, so soon past, so yesterday.

7) After all, it is not every year I can participate in a new reformation of Your Church. Lord, you must have loved the patristics. I do. So wise, so much closer to Your own walking. So far removed from these times of over-constricting reason.

8) So much to do...yet Lord, please keep my mind humble, protect me from the powerful rightness that so easily consumes all, over which it towers in arrogance.

9) I think, Lord, that I have stopped wondering why You have spared me so long. There is little point in the pot asking the potter why have You made me thus.

10) Now, as I look ahead, there are no milestones, no celebrations to accomplish, no "once-in-a-lifetime" birthdays, just every "once-in-a-lifetime" day. Each day new, every single morning offering new scope for what I never dared nor could have imagined might be. Every day a stunning miracle of Grace.

11) When I sleep, You are there. When I awake, even several times a day, You are there. When I rise up, which I can now, alone, without much help, You are there. If I make my bed in misery, You are there. When I sleep in peace. You are there. Such thoughts are too wonderful.

12) So, Lord, that was my ninety-ninth year. Truth be told, I did not want it when it began. Now it's done, I think I will have a few more, if You don't mind. Outside my window are the mountains that stretch down to the sea. Across my room lies the bed from which I will likely return to You when You call me home.

13) Until then, I have books to read, friends to welcome, letters to try and write—not so well anymore—my children and colleagues to call and encourage, reflections to reflect, and ponderings to ponder. And it is good. It is very, very good.

14) Lord, my Lord, how excellent is Your name in all the earth!

Letter #42

September 1, 2022

Dear friends,

As I have been reflecting on the wonder of Christ as our healer, I'm reminded of how resistant God's people were to His promises. Moses, whom God used to deliver Israel out of Egypt, was powerless to heal the emotional wounds of the Israelites. The prophets, minor and mighty, were equally unsuccessful. I'm reminded of the children's joke: "How many psychiatrists does it take to change a light bulb? Just one, but it really has to want to be changed!" Yet even desire does not seem to be enough—as we see the psalmist David, who cried out in deep distress to express that he found no experience of the Divine Physician. Indeed, all that David was experiencing emotionally was a deep loneliness, that God had hidden His face from him, and was ignoring him, had forsaken him. David felt just "skin and bones...like a desert owl," and when awake, "like a bird alone on a roof," as one who had come to the ending of his days, that had become but an "evening shadow," where he "withered away as grass" (Ps. 102:5-7, 11)—like so many desperate patients in our hospitals at the height of the pandemic, on stretchers, in hallways, alone, unattended, some dying alone simply for lack of capacity. In many ways, this was the state of Israel under the law; there was simply no way for the deep healing required. A brand-new covenant was required.

So many of us live like the psalmist, convinced we have been abandoned by God, left alone in the crowded but lonely corridors of our lives, in arid relationships, in tepid careers, in broken families—like the bleaching whale bones that sometimes wash up on the beach outside my window, that cling to a form of life that the heat of the sun has leached away. Even the promise of the dried bones in the desert to the prophet Ezekiel could not bring the restoration of God's people. It needed a new covenant, in the incarnation of the Son of God. Jesus,

His beloved son, could heal. Christ, indeed, is the universal healer, the eternal physician. As His followers, we often forget that He told us why He came. Standing in the Temple in Nazareth, amidst all the adults who knew him as a boy and a carpenter's son, He declares to us:

> The Spirit of the Lord is on me,
> because he has anointed me
> to proclaim good news to the poor.
> He has sent me to proclaim freedom for the prisoners
> and recovery of sight for the blind,
> to set the oppressed free,
> to proclaim the year of the Lord's favor.
> (Luke 4:18-19)

The very name Jesus (Yeshua) means "the Lord who saves." Translated from the Greek, it means "the Lord who delivers" or "saves life," or "heals" from death. Luke, himself a physician, records the text above, quoted when Jesus visited his childhood community at Nazareth, where he commenced his public ministry. What follows in Christ's life is a cavalcade of healings: a demon-possessed man is exorcised, a woman with high fever is healed, and after a long day healing, no doubt now very weary, "at sunset, the people brought to Jesus all who had various kinds of sickness, and laying his hands upon them, he healed them" (Luke 4:40). With scarcely any sleep, Jesus was up early, for "at daybreak, Jesus went out to a solitary place. The people were looking for him, and when they came to where he was, they tried to keep him from leaving them" (Luke 4:42) Jesus had grown up in the area. It was there that—born of a virgin—he was himself free of ancestral "sin" or "disease." Yet in being truly human, he shared in the cultural diseases then common. The early Fathers were profoundly in worship that the Creator of the universe was now identified with his creature, man, in all their afflictions. Jesus shared empathy with the sick, as he too experienced our bodily sicknesses. The Orthodox church especially, by their rites and ceremonies, have reflected mystically on how Christ will present all his redeemed to his father in heaven, "spirit, soul and body...kept blameless at the coming of our Lord Jesus Christ" (1 Thess. 5:23). The cause of sin was the disobedience of our first parents, and the healing of our souls now is in the obedience of Jesus to his heavenly father, so deeply expressed in John's gospel—"So if the Son sets you free, you will be free indeed" (John 8:36). Yet, we choose so often the desert, to wander, hungry.

Over the years, I have learned one place, at least, where I can enter under the touch of the Great Healer. It requires that I do nothing at all. I simply need to go to sleep. When I sleep, the keyboard must stop, my eyes cannot read, my mouth cannot speak, my thoughts become silent. Something in me stops and enters a place of complete dependence. Here in the hospital, there are some who struggle with inviting sleep. Like butterflies that never settle, activity camouflages a deep sadness that resists sleep. Yet that is where we find deep healing. Every day, I practice a desire to know the healing touch of the Great Physician and, with the hymn writer, to pray...

> Dear Lord and father of mankind,
> forgive our foolish ways:
> reclothe us in our rightful mind;
> in purer lives thy service find,
> in deeper reverence, praise.
>
> In simple trust like theirs who heard
> beside the Syrian sea
> the gracious calling of the Lord,
> let us like them, without a word,
> rise up and follow thee.
>
> O Sabbath rest, by Galilee!
> O calm of hills above,lwhere Jesus knelt to share with thee
> the silence of eternity,
> interpreted by love!
>
> Drop thy still dews of quietness,

till all our strivings cease;
take from our souls the strain and stress,
and let our ordered lives confess
the beauty of thy peace.

Breathe through the heats of our desire
thy coolness and thy balm;
let sense be dumb, let flesh retire,
speak through the earthquake, wind, and fire,
O still small voice of calm.[35]

May it be so, this day, for each of you.

In friendship,

Jim

Letter #43

Editor's Note: Dad has been rather prolific of late. As if he is somehow getting younger every day! And your faithful scribe is occasionally challenged to stay up with the emerging themes which tend to emanate, as beckoning an epic voyage on some discovery, only to be displaced, a few days later, by a new and equally inter-galactic intellectual odyssey. Readers of The Wind in the Willows, by Kenneth Graham, will recall the moment when Toad's zeal for the caravan is quite remarkably replaced by an equal zeal for the motor car, and all thought of the caravan seems quite so very "yesterday." Imagine trying to craft a transportation strategy for Toad! Considerable agility is required. Yet, amidst the recent flurry of emails on our next subject—to be "heavenly minded"—I found this gem, in its usual un-polished state. Close by my home, our local university is gearing up and grandkids are off to schools, and much that is new is starting. Amidst all this newness, this prayerful anchor in ancient words, full of wisdom for today, seems timely.

September 8, 2022

Dear friends,

Some ten or more years ago, I was led by the Lord to spend half the year on daily study and meditation on the Lord's Prayer. In my prayer time this morning, I felt urged to write my next letter on this theme. Rather like singing the national anthem of our country, the Lord's Prayer is so familiar to us that paradoxically, it has become so unfamiliar to us as Christians.

The prayer is reported in both Matthew 6:9-15 and Luke 11:1-4, with slight variants.

"Our Father in heaven"

God has spoken to us twice: firstly, through the reality of the earthly world and the cosmos—"the heavens declare..."—and secondly, through the prayer of his incarnate beloved son, who has, in His unfathomable self-emptying, made it possible for us to pray this prayer, as our mediator between God and mankind. I wonder, sometimes, what He makes of our babble in church when He has given us words to speak to Him. Sometimes, we use any other words but those He has given us to use. Rather, we need the heart of Hannah in her prayer:

> There is no one holy like the Lord:
> there is no one beside you;
> there is no Rock like our God.
> Do not keep talking so proudly,
> or your mouth speak such arrogance,
> for the Lord is a God who knows,
> and by him deeds are weighed.
> (1 Sam. 2:2-3)

The early Fathers recognized that the Lord's Prayer is far more than an expression of human earthly need, for it is expressed to become Christ-like instead of remaining like Adam, still rebellious against God. It is rather like becoming like Adam and Eve in the garden before their rebellious lapse into sin. It is like Jacob's ladder into heaven. It is like seeking to be restored to that pre-lapsed state when Adam and Eve communed with God in the garden.

"Hallowed be your name"

God gave man the power to "name the animals," but as God's creatures, we dare not name God. All language then about God can only be metaphorical. But by God's grace he gave us the privilege, as the "imago Dei," to commune with Him. As His people. Because of Christ's self-emptying—to become as a little child—we can now name "Jesus" as only a little child can do. The over-familiarity we sometimes practice in our speech is sheer blasphemy. Matthew picks this up in his gospel, in chapter 18, in declaring that as his disciples we have become as little children, for such is the kingdom of heaven. For holy indeed is His name, for by His name we can be "born-again," that is to have a transformed mind-set, to be completely other than we were. Such power in His name!

"Your kingdom come"

Like Hannah, we now enter the school of humility and obedience to the sovereign will of God. We are learning what the apostle Paul taught his son in the faith, Timothy, "for there is one God and one mediator between God and mankind" (1 Tim. 2:5). It is not Paul who is the great theologian, but it is Jesus Christ who is "the unique theologian," because He exemplified by His life, passion, and resurrection what Christian theology is all about. It is just "doctrine" if we only know it in an abstract way, but when it is lived, by inviting Christ's life to be expressed in us, all comes alive!

"Your will be done"

Uniquely, it was Jesus who in the Garden of Gethsemane, in his deep agony of prayer to the Father said, "nevertheless, not my will but thine be done." As Maximus the Confessor, one of the early Fathers (579-662), observed, Christ is the embodiment of selflessness. Not only did "the unique theologian" teach us the gospel, but in living and praying the gospel He, through His words in us, introduces us into the deep mysteries of our own faith. By this, our whole minds are transformed.

"On earth as it is in heaven"

The Lord's Prayer is stretching us between heaven and earth. We truly need to become "heavenly minded." Here we need to pause and pray with Thomas á Kempis, who baked and cooked for his house church, all done in the presence of the Lord: "Most gracious Jesus, grant me Your grace, I pray. Let it live and work in me and stay in me until the end. Grant me the will and desire to do always what is most pleasing and acceptable to You. Let Your will be mine and let my will always follow and be conformed totally to Your own."[36]

"Give us each day/today our daily bread"

St. Maximus continues: "The logos enables us to participate in the divine life by making Himself our food, in a manner understood by Himself and by those who have received from Him a noetic [or mindful] awareness of who God is."[37] As Psalm 145:8 declares, "The Lord is gracious and full of compassion," that is, full of mercy for all our daily needs.

"And lead us not into temptation but deliver us from evil (the evil one)"

It is our fallen nature to be tempt-able, as Adam and Eve fell into temptation, seduced by the serpent. Satan and "the evil one" should never be translated in personal terms, for that is the opposite of what they and demons are. They are all "things," seeking to de-personalize us, attempting to destroy our identity as the "imago Dei." Here Dante, in his classic poem, is our authority to see Satan frozen in a "lake," incapable of relating to itself, or to any human, or to God. To be tempted is to attempt to destroy our "imago Dei," so that we become a "thing" and not a person. It is the attempt to destroy our human and divine relationships by the madness of pride, gluttony, and other body-centered pre-occupations. It is what the Apostle Paul calls "the life of the flesh" (cf. Rom. 8).

Perhaps, when we have spoken again the words of our Lord, we might follow with those of St. Francis.

> Make me a channel of your peace; where there is hatred let me bring your love.
> Where there is injustice, your pardon Lord, and where there's doubt, true faith in you.
>
> Make me a channel of your peace, it is in pardoning that we are pardoned,
> and in dying that we're born to eternal life.
>
> Master, grant that I may never seek so much as to be consoled, as to console,
> to be understood, as to understand, to be loved, as to love with all my soul.[38]

May it be so for each one of you this week.

In friendship,

Jim

Letter #44

September 11, 2022

Dear friends,

Through a recent conversation with my daughter Claire, and in light of the seemingly sudden death of our Queen, I am prompted to share with you my own brief reflections on her life, on the occasion of her death. It was never my personal privilege to meet her in person, but I recall three "close encounters": Her life touched that of a dear friend and colleague, my own sister met her, and I had a personal encounter with her husband, the late Duke of Edinburgh. Three "close encounters" and through them, three lessons that I find both timely and instructive.

In the first, my good and now departed friend, John Stott, was invited by the Queen to provide her with personal counsel and instruction regarding her own faith in Christ. While John spoke very little of these regular meetings with Her Majesty, they originated from a well-publicized meeting she had with Billy Graham. It is reported that upon a request to suggest from whom else the Queen might seek personal counsel in her faith in Christ, Billy Graham had suggested she consult with John Stott. Today, she might have well sought out either the Archbishop of York or Canterbury, Stephen Cottrell and Justin Welby respectively, whose vibrant and deep personal faith in Christ is evident to all. But my friend John was more of a "rarity" in his time and so he became, for a time, an advisor to the Queen in knowing Christ more personally. The Queen wanted to know Jesus better and set out to do so. Such an inquiry changed her life of faith.

The second encounter was between the Queen and my own sister, Ethel, upon the receipt of recognition to my sister for her service to the Law. Ethel had first served her country in Bletchley, decoding military signals and abiding a life of deep secrecy. Later, Ethel went on to become the first female in Scottish history to be a law partner in a

Scottish law firm, and to serve on a number of royal commissions. In receiving an OBE (Order of the British Empire), Ethel was the recipient of an award that derived from the institutionalizing of commendation, of saying "well done," of an act to call forth and offer praise to another. This action, steeped as it is in precedent, was important enough to the Queen that she showed up and said "well done" to my sister. She didn't have to, but it matters. She went out of her otherwise busy schedule and stopped, looked at Ethel, and told her she had done a good job. It makes me wonder how many of us do the same. Do we notice what others have done that is good? Do we go out of our way to simply affirm, to congratulate, to praise, to add a voice of appreciation for their actions? Perhaps we should do that more.

The third encounter was my own, when the Duke of Edinburgh visited the newly constructed College of St. Catherine's in Oxford, where I was a tutor. The new building was proudly on display with its Danish architect present, fussing over everything that the Duke should appreciate. Like many Danish lowland structures, the college is built almost below the level of the Isis River, a tributary to the Thames. On the day of his visit, it was wet, very wet, and the bemused Duke expressed his hope that the new building would not sink into the mire! It was not that the late Duke was any stranger to rigor. Indeed, he was a strong supporter of his own alma mater, Gordonstoun, where the founder had brought a pedagogy that involved a close interaction of both physical and intellectual rigor. Both the Queen and her husband, despite all their worldly "power," recognized that they needed to be in submission to something other than themselves. In a recent television interview, a grieving subject repeated a few times her admiration for "the most powerful woman in the world," and while that may well be hyperbole, there is undeniably a dimension of the lives of both the Queen and her husband that, despite their titles and considerable wealth, they have lived in submission to a rigor that was not of their wills, but of another and greater will than their own.

Three "close encounters" with a monarch now dead. Three principles: to know Jesus better, to bless and affirm others, and to submit our wills to a rigor greater than our own authority. Quite the woman, quite the legacy. We might do well to follow her example in these ways, such that when we are dead others might reflect of us that we desired to know Christ more, were liberal with praise, and placed our autonomy under the yoke of obedience. May it be said of us all.

In friendship,

Jim

Letter #45

Editor's note: The theme of our next few letters, I think, will be what Dad has referred to as being "heavenly minded." For those of his readers who knew my mother and his wife, Rita, you may not find it hard to imagine that the term "heavenly minded" quickly conjures memories of her Glaswegian burr intoning her perspective on those "so heavenly minded that they were no earthly good"! It has required of your scribe a discipline to persist beyond the mischievous banter and either/or orientation of my Mum (which she herself did not in reality practice, but it made a good one liner) and dig deeper into the meaning of what Dad is actually on about. He has himself described various stages of experiencing the thinning of the "veil," as he would put it, and while his age helps to prescribe a certain preparedness for heaven, I think he is encouraging us to live now in two realities, one of which is bound by space and time and the other of which is not.

September 15, 2022

Dear friends,

In these past weeks, I have been reflecting on the significance of our need as Christians to live as those who are "heavenly minded." In my letter in which we reflected on much of the Lord's Prayer, I was struck again by the invitation from Jesus for us to live aware of two realities, "on earth, as it is in heaven" (Matt. 6:10). Actually, Jesus instructs his followers, through that prayer we are to use, to invoke the will of God in two realms, on earth and in heaven, both at the same time. But what does this mean?

C.S. Lewis, writing in *Mere Christianity,* said: "If you read history you will find that the Christians who did most for the present world were just those who thought most of the next...It is since Christians have largely ceased to think of the other world that they have become so ineffective in this."[39] Jesus promised His disciples before His ascension into glory: "My Father's house has many rooms; if that were not so, would I have told you that I am going there to prepare a place for you" (John 14:2), which we might interpret as God having many realms of reality. Indeed, as Creator of all realms of reality, God intends us to live in more than one sense of reality. Since we bear His image, as "imago Dei"— while we might find that immensely challenging—we are already wired, as it were, to do so.

My son Chris has recently been describing to me his visits to his gym. As many of my friends well know, athleticism is not a family trait, but Chris is learning from my own aging experience that sustaining movement is critical. As his instructor intones, "motion is lotion." In his classes, what proves most challenging is to apply intentionality to the movement of specific muscles so that they move in ways he intends rather than as they have become accustomed through lack of use. He reports the frequent experience that asking certain movements of certain muscles is akin to meeting old friends with whom you have long since lost touch. Gone is the familiarity of interaction between mind and body that made childhood movements so fluid. Old connections must once again be discovered so that they can be re-activated. Similarly, many of us have lost the child-like ease with which we lived by faith, and become overly dependent on our very limited sight.

Many commentators have reflected that the rise of science through the Enlightenment disabused the parishioner of the threat of "eternal damnation" or the promise of "heaven," and so accelerated the rise of secularism, which today only further advances. When "conversion" was seen as some kind of "celestial plane ticket" to glory, the notion was quickly debunked by even simple science, much less the more sophisticated astrophysics and molecular biology of the late twentieth century. As a teenager, I recall the horror of being invited by the father of one of my friends to join them at a "night show" accompanied by the assurance that all was OK because we had our "tickets to heaven" and so could act with impunity on earth. Such "faith" was sheer lunacy. It is perhaps just as well that we do not know the confessions of "christians" with such thinking.

As a real human being, and yet also the unique Son of God, Jesus revealed his dual identity in the earthly experience of the transfiguration. Strangely, in all my life of almost a century, I have rarely heard a sermon preached on the transfiguration. In this hyper-scientific age, it is an awkward text. What do we do with it? Do we avoid it, as Lewis suggested, because we have so little interest in the next realm of reality? Yet the apostle Luke, the well-trained physician, does so both in his Gospel and in the Acts of the Apostles. From his experience of hearing the report of the transfiguration from the three disciples, and having experienced himself the event of Pentecost, Luke's report on the transfiguration seeks to unite the two natures of Jesus Christ as "the Lord of Heaven and earth." Origen (c.185-253), one of the most learned of the early Fathers, comments on this, as he succinctly describes Jesus Christ's two natures, as both human (Jesus) and divine (Christ). "Those with glory appeared in glory to the disciples. Moses showed the face of the Law, and Elijah showed the face of the prophets. Jesus himself was Lord of the Law, and of the prophets. So, whoever understands the spiritual law and the wisdom hidden in mystery in the prophets, sees Moses and Elijah in glory."[40] He goes on, "and they conversed with each other—that is, they said things that are in mutual agreement." Origen clearly joins the men of the Old Covenant to the apostles because, at the second coming of Christ, all will be joined together.

In his report of the transfiguration, Luke tells us in Chapter 9 that when Peter heard Jesus was going to suffer—and he did not want that to happen—thinking he had found the right time and place, he asked the Lord to remain always above (i.e. hidden on the mountain), lest the Jews find him and kill him. Origen, in his interpretation of Luke's report, recognizes that Peter does not know the good things that will come from the Passion and the Resurrection, for all men. He writes,

> As he said this, a cloud put an end to their eagerness to seek something beyond their power. Through this event he prefigures the truth that all the saints—both those before the Lord's coming, and those after his coming—will be together. The Law and the prophets and the Gospel will set up the same

> tents—three in number—but looking toward one goal. At the Resurrection, the saints will be 'taken upon the clouds to meet the Lord and to be with Him forever.[41]

For me, at this stage of my life, the message of this transfiguration narrative—an event where the pressing needs of the moment that Peter senses are held in such tension with the enormity of God's redemptive intervention in human history—this message is highly instructive. Both realities have an urgency. Both have their own clarity. Both are equally intense and real. This is where Christ invites us to live our lives, like the sailor in his hammock at sea, slung between the two anchors of the "already" and the "not yet." That we should be confused and moved in practical ways, as Peter was, seems only to be human. That we should have steely clarity as Christ facing the cross, is to allow the imago Dei that burns within us all to resolve "not my will, but thine." To be heavenly minded is not to live pushing non-scientific delusions; it is to respond to live in both realities, heaven and earth.

Oliver Wendell Holmes (1809-1910), who was—like the Apostle Luke—a medical practitioner and indeed, Professor of Medicine at Harvard Medical School, composed this hymn in 1848:

> Lord of all being, throned afar, Thy glory flames from sun and star:
> Centre and soul of every sphere, Yet to each loving heart how near!
>
> Sun of our life, thy quickening ray Sheds on our path the glow of day;
> Star of our hope, thy softened light Cheers the long watches of the night.
>
> Our midnight is thy smile withdrawn, Our noontide is thy gracious dawn.
>
> Our rainbow arch thy mercy's sign; All, save the clouds of sin, are Thine.

> Lord of all life, below, above, Whose light is truth, whose warmth is love,
> Before thy ever-blazing throne, We ask no lustre of our own.
>
> Grant us thy truth to make us free, And kindling hearts that burn for Thee,
> Till all Thy living altars claim, One holy light, one heavenly flame.[42]

My prayer for each of you is that as you are, like the Apostle Peter, caught up in the enormous demands of the very real practical exigencies of your lives, that you might sense and respond to Christ's persistent invitation to also join Him, beyond the mere boundaries of space and time, in a reality where Love reigns supreme and that so anchored, your engagement here might all the more fruitful be.

In friendship,

Jim

Letter #46

September 15, 2022

Dear friends,

As we continue to consider what it means, in practice, to be "heavenly minded," I'd like to share with you a glimpse into my days and how they generally begin. After finishing breakfast with my fellow denizens on this part of the second floor of our hospital, friends whom I refer to as fellow "inmates," I return to my comfortable chair which is beside a large window overlooking a beautiful park. I have the leisure in my retirement *[Editor's note: ...What retirement!! He certainly keeps the rest of us busy enough!]*, to ask myself, "What shall I do this morning?" "Doing something" is the role of Martha, "filled with many cares" instead of emulating Mary "sitting at the Lord's feet" in contemplation. I am privileged to be one floor up looking down upon a small park still populated with a few remaining trees that are part of the old-growth forests that once filled this modern cityscape. Always an explorer, I was asking the Lord how we could together explore in this next series of meditations and how could you and I become more of a healing "presence" in the lives of others. For, in the pristine state of contemplation, when the nature of being human was to be made in the image and likeness of God, Adam and Eve—and thence you and I—were all created by God in His image and likeness, to have positive emotions like kindness, mercy and indeed to love one another. I am reminded of Christ's declaration in Luke 4 of His mission to preach good news to the poor, give sight to the blind and release for the captives, and set the oppressed at liberty. All specific acts of service and healing for others.

Spiritual knowledge or contemplation, stated the early Fathers, was the end of praxis or practice, as St. Maximus observed: "as contemplation, becoming the healing of the emotions, leading to our fuller conversion."[43] The ascetic life contributed to this new condition of contemplation, as "cleansing of the soul." The two must now go together, practice and contemplation. Faith, and its practice in helping others, go together. Martha is action without contemplation, while Mary's posture was the better role, of contemplation at the feet of Jesus, who accomplishes everything for us. In marriage or in friendship, if one partner is only a facilitator, like Martha, then if the other is only a server, or exhorter, or perceiver, then there could develop tensions between them. But the "better part," as Jesus mildly rebuked Martha, was the posture of Mary as a contemplative. None of us ever really get this balance between action and contemplation right. Even with limited mobility, I find the urgency to write before reflection still haunts me nearly every day, so I have to lean towards too much contemplation because I will easily drift towards too much (attempted, at least) action.

So, as I began my morning today, I asked myself, how is it possible I can become a healing—indeed, a truly "therapeutic"—presence, in the lives of one or more persons who are already "in Christ," to use the Apostle Paul's language? I am quite certain that it does not begin with being busy; rather, it begins with being still. It begins with being "heavenly minded" that I might through deeper contemplation become more "earthly good."

As contemplation becomes the healer of every ill, so we sing with Marty Haughen:

> Healer of our every ill,
> light of each tomorrow,
> give us peace beyond our fear,
> and hope beyond our sorrow.
>
> In the pain and joy beholding
> how your grace is still unfolding,
> give us all your vision, God of love.
>
> You who know each thought and feeling,
> teach us all your way of healing;

Spirit of compassion, fill each heart.[44]

My prayer for you this week is that as you choose stillness over action, contemplation over neglect, and meditation over thoughtlessness, the Lord will soften your heart for others, will bring them to mind such that you can then bring them before Christ and deepen your desire that they be healed. May He then grant you the desires of your heart, His desires in your heart.

In friendship,

Jim

Letter #47

September 29, 2022

Dear friends,

As we continue to reflect further on what it means for us to be "heavenly minded," I would like to explore a little of a pattern of choice that I continue to find rather challenging, personally, but which should, by this stage in life, be much easier. The choice is one of stillness.

I confess to a certain irony that in my sense of urgency and even drive to prepare a letter for you each week, in searching for new topics to explore, that stillness remains elusive even when so much of my body is hardly adequate for vigorous physical activity. Thus, first of all, when I speak of stillness, I am not referring to a state of being motionless, even though that might help. Were being without motion sufficient for stillness, I should know much more about the subject in practice than I find that I do. Even on days when my enthusiasm for mobility of any kind wanes, I find stillness to be an ongoing challenge. Many teach that to be truly still, our minds must be at rest and in a sense, even empty of thought—but the early Fathers of our church had much deeper insight that we have perhaps lost.

One of the reasons that I have spent so much time in my career seeking to engage with the early Fathers of the church is that they lived their lives so much nearer to the world of Christ's apostles. My children tease me that some of my very best friends have been dead for nearly two millennia, and it is likely true. Early in my career as a Geographer, in Oxford, I was introduced to writings that were later compiled into several volumes of *The Philokalia,* edited by G.E.H. Palmer, Philip Sherrard, and Kallistos Ware. There I learned of the word *hesychia,* which I came to understand as being cleansed of bad thoughts. As I sleep and cannot control my thoughts, I have learned to invite the Lord to guard my mind as I sleep and so to dwell peacefully in His presence.

Far from a vacant mind, the stillness to which Christ invites us is the kind of stillness that he sought out Himself. John Michael Talbot, the musician, has written that "those who wanted to follow Jesus wanted to imitate his stillness before they could imitate his actions. They needed to understand his silence before they could speak his words. They needed to know his emptying of self through ultimate dying before they could proclaim the abundance of eternal life."[45] This kind of stillness is active, not passive. It not the stillness of the vacant mind; it is a deep stillness that is the corollary for the vigorous action that lies ahead. It is one of active mental quietude, not an embrace of dead silence but of active listening for the God who speaks. This is the stillness of Samuel, who says to the Lord, "Speak, for your servant is listening" (1 Sam. 3:10).

This stillness we need to seek is to actively embrace a willingness to be taught by God, as Matthew the apostle writes, "seek first his kingdom…" (Matt. 6:33). To be "heavenly minded" is not to have a vacant and or passive mind; it is to have the mind of Christ. As the apostle Paul urges us, "Let this mind be in you which was also in Christ Jesus," which Paul describes as a mind of humility, of active attention to the Father, of being stilled from all distractions so that we can hear His voice and attend to His will, one of being emptied of self (Phil. 2:5-8).

From a convent in Germany, in the 18th century, a little-known nun, Catharina von Schlegel, penned these words that may inspire our hearts…

> Be still, my soul; the Lord is on your side;
> bear patiently the cross of grief or pain;
> leave to your God to order and provide;
> in ev'ry change he faithful will remain.
> Be still, my soul; your best, your heav'nly friend
> through thorny ways leads to a joyful end.
>
> Be still, my soul; your God will undertake
> to guide the future as he has the past;

your hope, your confidence, let nothing shake;
all now mysterious shall be bright at last.
Be still, my soul; the waves and winds still know
his voice who ruled them while he lived below.

Be still, my soul; when dearest friends depart
and all is darkened in the vale of tears,
then you will better know his love, his heart,
who comes to soothe your sorrows and your fears.
Be still, my soul; your Jesus can repay
from his own fullness all he takes away.

Be still, my soul; the hour is hast'ning on
when we shall be forever with the Lord,
when disappointment, grief, and fear are gone,
sorrow forgot, love's purest joys restored.
Be still my soul; when change and tears are past,
all safe and blessed we shall meet at last.[46]

What strikes me about this hymn is how it illustrates that stillness is a gift, not of our wrestling, but for our receiving. May we each find the space and time in which we might receive such a gift knowing that through its receiving we, with Christ, are thus prepared for whatever lies ahead.

In friendship,

Jim

Letter #48

October 6, 2022

Dear friends,

As we continue to wonder what it means for us to be "heavenly minded," I'd like to explore an antithesis to help us see more clearly, literally. Many of us suffer from a profound "spiritual blindness" that most certainly interferes with any capacity to be "heavenly minded."

The human eye, like the other parts of the body, is in and of itself inert, as if it were part of a cadaver. The eye sees, but it does not interpret what it sees. As modern science arose, we invented in the16th century spectacles, microscopes, and telescopes. Each could aid the eye to see what it might not otherwise see. By observing the polestar, fixed in the heavens, ships could purposefully navigate the oceans, while the microscope allowed us to observe tiny forms of life, now even germs with more modern electron microscopes. Yet despite this remarkable capacity for vision and its enhancement, all would be a blur in the sky, in using a telescope—or a blur of many germs, in using a microscope—without knowing what one is looking for.

My son Chris, drawing on his post-graduate studies in biology, reminded me of an important dynamic of predator/prey relationships. For example, the large insect, the praying mantis, forms in its cones of its eye what biologists call a "searching image." This is a pattern of the prey for which the insect is in search. As a result, when they see and recognize their prey, they respond more quickly and significantly increase their ability to catch that prey before it escapes. Similarly, if you have lost a ring on your carpet, it is much easier to find if you know what it looks like. We see better when we are looking for something!

Some years ago, I was fortunate to find a doctor who had the skills to remove my cataracts and give me new lenses for my eyes. It may well be the most frequently performed surgery of any kind, and many of you may well have experienced its remarkable benefits. Yet, these benefits are so much more enhanced because we know what we are looking for and we know very well what it means to see clearly. So too, we may need our "spiritual cataracts" to be removed. These spiritual and often emotional wounds dull our vision, blur our ability to see with hope, and impede our capacity to see "heaven on earth."

When Peter, James and John were privileged to be invited to behold Jesus' glory on the Mount of the Transfiguration, it was, indeed, a uniquely glorious sight. But Peter remained blind to the exalted glory of Jesus, wanting to find a cave where he could hide Jesus from being found by his persecutors, and doubtless where he could hide himself also. For the Miocene chalk hills and mounts of Israel, such as at the Mount of the Transfiguration, are full of caverns. Peter remained spiritually blind to the Messianic identity and meaning of the name of Jesus. So on another occasion, Luke reports that Jesus explained why He speaks in parables: "so that, though seeing, they may not see; though hearing, they may not understand" (Luke 8:10).

These days, when there is far more that I cannot do than I can, I find myself very dependent on the few capacities that I have left. And yet, while still blessed with sight, I still find that I can be blind. Even with my powerful hearing aids (if I put them on, my children will say!), I can still remain quite deaf to what the Lord may want me to hear. I need not only to open my eyes and my ears but to look with intention to see, to sense, to catch a glimpse of the Spirit of God moving. And when I look intently and I invite the Lord to remove my spiritual cataracts, to heal my emotions that blur my vision, what I see is a wonder of Grace. I see what Pilgrim saw as he peered across the river at the Heavenly City; I see what Isaiah saw when he saw "the Lord, high and lifted up, and His train filled the temple."

For us Christians today (this means until the day of our death), we have to keep going forward, seeing and hearing new insights of our blessed relationship with our Lord. As we have said many times in these letters, we need to frequently have new "Nicodemus" experiences, of "being born again."

So we sing again in our hearts, as we have done before:

> Open my eyes Lord, Help me to see your face, Open my eyes Lord.
>
> Open my ears Lord, Help me to hear your voice, Open my ears Lord.
>
> Open my heart Lord, Help me to love like you, Open my heart Lord.
>
> I live within you, Deep in your heart, I live within you.[47]

In friendship,

Jim

Letter #49

Editor's note: It is quite remarkable that in the weeks that your scribe fails to produce a letter on time and finds himself pre-occupied with matters others than faithfully interpreting Dad's reflections, that many write to see how he is. Remarkably, while the rest of us, his children in particular, find themselves aging gracefully in the manner to which most of us are accustomed, Dad just keeps on getting younger. We are alarmed at how these trajectories might play out over time. Rest assured that any interruption in letters is not related to failing health, just his fragile support system! Thank you for your concerns for his welfare, but as he approaches his 100th birthday on November 21, his vigour is increasing!

October 20, 2022

Dear friends,

I have been reflecting of late on the subject of "Christian Fellowship," made all the more relevant as we find such darkening of the times. In our worst moments of fear, we are inclined towards "huddling together" as in a reflex of mutual support. The early Christians in catacombs and the bombed victims of the Blitz in London drew comfort from their interdependence, just as we see such bravery in young girls in the streets of Tehran. Yet it seems as if what we might call Christendom is becoming much more fragmented, at the very times when cohesion and real fellowship are all the more vital, as darker times are here and darkening still. I have been pondering why this might be so and how we might encourage one another.

Some years ago, I was exploring what it means to live in friendship with God. Abraham was called a friend of God, as also were Isaac and then Moses. This is language we don't use today. People do not make claim to being a "friend of God." We might think it strange if they did! To be a "friend of God" is simply to trust Him, fully, and live in obedience to His Word, the same Word that brought creation into being. Jesus, at the Last Supper, as He prepared for the cross said to His disciples, "You are my friends, if you do what I command" (John 15:14). The apostle Peter, even though he had seen the glory of the Lord at the transfiguration, broke that friendship when he did not want Jesus arrested—and later, when he denied his friend. This kind of intimacy that I am calling "friendship" disappears from the life of the Church in the writing of the Desert Fathers, as they focused first on asceticism and their hermetic life, but reappears later.

In the beginning of the 14th century, a remarkable German mystic, Rulman Merswin, wrote among other writings, the parables of human relationships called *The Book of Nine Rocks.* It describes the nature of nine categories of society from the ruling class to the poor, all contributing to the alienation of "Christendom." Many of you will be relieved that I will refrain from sharing the details of all nine rocks (much as I find them fascinating!) but each represents stages or places we might "inhabit" on our journey to a deeper life in Christ. Of the ninth rock and most to be desired, he writes that it is "more necessary to Christendom than everything else written in this book. The reason is that if anyone decides to join the company of those on the rock, he will be dearer to God and help Christendom more than a thousand other men [and women] who live on the lower rocks and who are disobedient and live after their own self-will."[48] Those who live on the ninth rock "are 'the righteous,'" who truly pray to God in spirit and in truth."

From our human perspective, the true binding force that holds Christendom or "Christian Fellowship" together is our own deepening friendship with God such that we become "dearer to God" with each passing day. This now is more and more my desire to simply be His friend, to become dearer to Him and to know that intimacy. Out of that place of deeper and deeper dependence, not from my projects, but from my friendship, I can offer to others in Christian Fellowship a richness that my activity could never yield.

More recently, the English hymnist Fred Pratt Green has written...

> The Church of Christ in every age beset by change but Spirit led,
> Must claim and test its heritage and keep on rising from the dead.

> Then let the servant Church arise, a caring Church that longs to be
> A partner in Christ's sacrifice, and clothed in Christ's humanity.
>
> We have no mission but to serve in full obedience to our Lord:
> To care for all, without reserve, and to spread his liberating Word.[49]

My prayer for us all is that we each seek such friendship with God that our lives can the more fully strengthen the bonds of Christendom in these darkening times in which we live.

In friendship,

Jim

Letter #50

October 27, 2022

Dear friends,

Last week I wrote about Christendom—a word we usually associate with something good—and I'd like to explore a deeper and more insidious dimension against which we must be on our guard. When Christendom is the kingdom of God's reign on earth, we are blessed, but when it becomes the guise for humanity's reign over God's people, we hamper God's kingdom rather than advance it. Sadly, the disease is subtle and invasive, for it revolves around our relationship with power and above all, human reason.

The more I study and read the writings of the early saints of the church, those we refer to as the "patristics"—both male and female—the more I see the disadvantages that we must overcome, derived from nearly two millennia of human thought. The early followers of Christ were simply closer to the New Testament narrative than we, especially in our post-Enlightenment embrace of reason as the predominant epistemology or way of knowing. Today, it is science that has become deified, and we have come to look on conversion as an event of the left hemisphere of our brain, as if we needed to be convinced by God to believe Him and His son Jesus, such that our faith becomes an assertion of a catechism or a belief in a statement about the Gospel. Once, we saw such passionate zeal for Christ that the early Christian martyrs were unafraid to face death by wild animals in the arena. Today, I am surrounded by dear people here, where I live, who are deeply afraid to face death because their reasoning offers a very insufficient depth of conviction. Across evangelicalism, our faith has become shallow and rote and even worse, political. Our church membership becomes just that, membership, and mainly just membership in a very human organization. Sadly—no, tragically—our too-adult minds only perceive the human structures and not the surging Life far below the surface of the organization we have "joined." And so we "church shop" like butterflies flitting from one brightly coloured flower to another in search of a quick taste of some nectar, any nectar. Like Nicodemus, we desperately need to be "born again," and again, and again.

One of the gifts that I have found in my much-later years has come to me through the loss of my dear wife Rita. With the confidence that she is in the Lord's presence, I find that the veil that separates me from my lifelong companion grows thinner. Because I know her so well, I am drawn closer to the place where Christ dwells and I see more and more of Him, even as I sense her closeness. It is like climbing a mountain, for I am constantly gaining new perspectives and insights of my salvation. Paul reminds us 68 times that our identity is "in Christ" and we are each called to be saints like Bernard of Clairvaux, like Teresa of Avila, and like von Balthasar and Adrienne von Speyr, who were only recently canonized. You can't think or reason your way into an identity, or convince yourself by repeating mere words. You simply inhabit it with your whole self.

Thankfully, there is a now a new movement of God's Spirit, inspiring new scholars to recover in patristic scholarship what "Fathers," like Origen in the second century A.D., speak of the Advent of the promised "Messiah": the Greatest Physician of all time, Jesus Christ, the Son of God. The Roman physician, the Apostle Luke, begins his letter with a dedication to "Theophilus," which means "lover of God." Luke is stating that only those seeking God as His lovers will make sense of what he is describing. The miraculous healings and parables that follow make sense when we embrace them as "lovers of God," not rationalists looking for cognitive explanations. Luke, despite his training, wants us to let the right sides of our brains loose, not just depend on the left's logic. This embrace of the early church writers is an embrace of our emotional identity in Christ, and the healing of those emotions in our worship, our joy, our lament, our devotion all so well expressed in the song book of the psalter.

My prayer for you is as W.P McKay wrote in the mid-19th century in the last verse of his hymn:

> Revive us again, fill each heart with thy love.
> May each soul be rekindled with fire from above.
>
> Hallelujah! Thine the glory, hallelujah! Amen!
> Hallelujah! Thine the glory, revive us again.[50]

In friendship,

Jim

Letter #51

November 3, 2022

Dear friends,

I confess that for very few days in my life did I ever imagine that I would be writing letters to friends, all over the world, in the month of November 2022, a century after the month of my birth. Like most good things in life, they are not planned. They just seem to show up with virtually no help from us at all, which makes the theme I now want to explore all the more vital. My focus now is gratitude.

Some years ago, my son Chris and I were teaching together in Brazil, at a conference of business leaders who also were followers of Christ. We had the opportunity to answer questions from the audience, and one was addressed to me by virtue of my age: "To what, Dr. Houston, do you attribute your long life?" Without much thought and with no reference to matters of nutrition or genes or an absence of unhealthy indulgence, I simply replied with one word, "gratitude!" I do not believe it was what was expected by my questioner, and I wonder what they took away from my response, which simply came from my heart and out of deep conviction.

As my children have each grown into adulthood, they have noticed that I spend very little of my life considering the past—my own past, that is—and no time wishing I were somehow transported back. They tease me that some of my best friends have been dead for millennia, and that is quite true...Origen, Augustine, Teresa, and long before them, the prophet Jeremiah caught my attention and affection as a young teen. But to reflect on and explore the past is not to live there, not to regret its losses, not to find the present and the future less compelling than some distant and now gone past. I think the practice of gratitude is what allows us to leave the past and its hurts, its wounds and even its joys as belonging to a past that is gone, and to anticipate a future that has not yet unfolded. Yet, some of us find the practice of gratitude deeply troubling because we are in such emotional pain from past wounds. Perhaps, if I might encourage you, the pursuit of gratitude and the revealing of its obstacles might lead you to places that need and can be healed by the Great Physician.

Our God has a remarkable quality that pertains to our need for gratitude: He makes all things new. Much of what we consider loss, once in His hands, becomes gain. Some of my deepest discouragements in the life of Regent were to become the source of new life. When I was fired as founding principal, I found a profound richness in the lives of so many students with whom I could now more freely interact, once relieved of administrative duties. Getting there was deeply painful, but it may have been one of the most life-giving transitions of my professional life. Loss with Christ is gain. Envy can beget gratitude. In a similar vein, I vividly remember leaving Oxford and my academic career in Geography—in which I had worked to seek for personal legitimacy, for over 30 years—only to barely hang on to a part-time lecturer post at UBC to augment our meagre income. Yet, out of what seemed to be at the time so emptying, there flowed a bounty for our family that today leaves me speechless. Loss with Christ was gain.

But it is not always that way. Sunshine does not always follow rain, such that we can easily give thanks with good reason. Today as I write, I know of deep struggles in the lives of many for whom I care, both within and outside my own family. Many in my place of residence are hampered in their practice of gratitude by the overwhelming sense of loss that being "old" has inflicted. There is much that I can no longer do that was once much easier or even possible at all. Yet the invitation still sounds to enter each day grateful for sleep, for breath itself, with a sense of what it is that is good, not what is missing, lost or even bad. There is something profoundly simple and yet essential in giving thanks for food before we eat. I hope, in some way, where you are in time and place, you can join me in simply giving thanks!

Brian Wren in his hymn of 1954 writes in the fifth verse,

> Thank you, God, for making planet earth
> a home for us, and ages yet unborn.
> Help us to share, consider, save and store.
> Come and renew the face of the earth.[51]

In friendship,

Jim

Letter #52

Editor's Note: An Epilogue from your scribe (This also appears, slightly modified, at the beginning of this work.)

November 3, 2022

Next week, the last letter in this series will be published, just a few days before Dad celebrates, with much of his family, his 100th birthday. We are currently planning a new genre, but a year ago, we set out to explore Dad's 100th year. It is now complete, and this series of letters will end next week. As a family, we began this journey in a very different place than we find ourselves today. In mid 2021, Dad had fallen, lost his mobility, and been hospitalized. In retrospect, he was probably not eating properly and slept a great deal during the day. His spirits were low, and he was quite certain that he just wanted to move to the "hospice" so he could follow Mum home, just as soon as the Lord could arrange it, preferably sooner. We wonder sometimes if he expected a chariot to appear like Elijah –"bring me my chariot of fire!"—but the Lord had other plans. Gradually, Dad began to want to read and to write again. My sister Claire and I needed to find a genre that would work for him without the appropriate rigors of academic publication.

Letters From a Hospital Bed began as a simple way to enable Dad to once again communicate what was on his heart…and then it just grew. When we first began, his notes were cryptic and mainly indecipherable, yet they contained gems that I recognized from decades of simply listening to what he thought. I recognized patterns and themes that were familiar but always with a new and urgent edge of growth. His more-than-occasional flights of fancy triggered another awareness—as I prepared each letter to send to Claire, who managed all the on-line engagement—the voice of our Mum chimed in, when earth seemed to have lost any grip on Dad and he needed to be "grounded" once again. And so, I invented these "Editor's notes" to provide a way for Mum to speak her piece from time to time, and occasionally burst a rather "heavenly minded" bubble that needed to be more "earthly good." Some weeks, Dad would send lots of notes and others he grew quiet and even silent. Gradually he wrote more and, most blessedly, began to make more sense, which helped the editing process considerably. His reading has become once again more voracious, and his once dispersed library is once again growing, rapidly, mainly with the books of very long-dead people!

Yet, as this letter project continued toward what is now some 50 letters and a mailing list that is well over 1000 friends around the world, something else happened in me, as I recrafted his notes into the letter genre we had together created. For many decades, Dad has been a feature in the lives of students and friends that number in the thousands. This has had a consequence for his children: He has been much less in our lives than in yours. It was not always easy sharing him with the regular household visitors, let alone through virtual means. Sometimes, as young adults, it was a real relief when he was busy with his teaching and lectures, but that independence wears thin after a while, and we have each listened to the enthusiasm of others for Dad's favour when we wondered if we might occasionally share it ourselves. For me as his son, this project has been redemptive in so many ways that I want simply to bear witness to that and encourage other parents and children to stay faithful to one another through what might be hard years. Sometimes the harvest of patience is long in coming, even taking nearly 70 years in the ripening.

We have all said of Dad's 100th year that in it he has grown steadily younger. He delights in his renewed mobility and his daily opportunity to tend to the needs of his caregivers. There is a lovely reciprocity at work that invites us each to consider how we might extend grace, in abundance, even from the growing limits of our own age and stage. He yearns to "stay faithful 'til the end." As your scribe, I have sought to be relentless in pursuit of "praxis" to Dad's "thesis," to demand that he encounter for himself the truth that he wished to convey. Sometimes, I think I quite mystified him with my insistence on needing to "live" his "theology" and to connect what he might be gleaning from a long-dead "patristic," some truth that might help us all deal with culture wars, or Ukraine, or climate change or pandemic or the myriad of harshening realities in a world busy abandoning God. Perhaps my insistence was purely selfish—I needed to know why something mattered, not just that it was interesting—but I hoped that I was representing you all faithfully in my asking. At one point he said, "You are asking me to write autobiographically. It is not what I do!" Perhaps I was, and to his considerable credit, after 99 years, he bent to this new task and learned still more. To have shaped my father, even as he has shaped me, brought the project full circle. It was done, and now it is time for something else.

With thanks to you all for your patient reading and to my sister Claire who made all the writing visible. You will find his birthday greeting to you all next week in our final posting in this series.

Your faithful scribe,

Chris

Letter #53

November 17, 2022

Dear friends,

In just a few days from now, on November 21st, I will celebrate my 100th birthday. My mother, to whom I was born when she was 40 years of age, had been told at the age of eighteen that she had but a few years to live. So much for prognostications about life expectancy! It seems her genes and those of my father were tougher than expected. But this milestone causes me to ask more than a few times, "Why did God spare me to now, to live for over a century instead of my 'allotment' of 'three score years and ten'?" I have outlived all my peer colleagues and nearly all my friends from my own generation—though clearly not any of you who are still reading my letters! Just over a year ago, I entered this hospital, also a hospice, where dear Rita had died and where I hoped to soon follow her. So certain and so eager was I to return to the Lord, that I gave my children instructions concerning my funeral arrangements, including the substitution for a traditional photograph of the version of Psalm 1 that I have shared with you before and is reproduced here.

The psalmist David uses this psalm as the entry point into the transparency of his heart before God, which unfolds through the poetry that follows. The image hangs before my table as I write, with the bed in which I will likely breathe my last on one side, and a window out to the adjacent park filled with vibrant life on the other. Here I sit before the psalm, slung between my own eternal rest and the continuity of life outside my window. The literary center of the psalm before me; its focus, its heart, is the simple word "fruit." Fruit that is borne by the well-rooted tree through the choices of one who follows the way of the righteous. A third of the poems that follow in the psalms are laments. Many psalms contain language that seems wholly inappropriate, even rude, unless they are being spoken, in deep distress and honesty, to a loving and personal God who really wants to hear what we say. This book, this Word, is where I choose to focus my attention as I give thanks for the grace of 100 years, such that it may one day be said that my life was fruitful.

Not until we arrive at the New Testament text do we really understand the nature of the fruitful life promised for the well-rooted tree. The Apostle Paul, writing his letter to the Philippians, describes what these fruits are: love, joy, peace, forbearance, kindness, goodness, faithfulness, and self-control. So that when we are in the presence of others, our "presence" can become "a therapeutic presence" for them. The early Fathers saw the fruits as being from the healing of our souls, that Jesus Christ has become our Eternal Physician and through His healing of us, we become bearers of the fruit of His Spirit. None of us yet are fully "healed," but the journey to "soul health" is now in progress, until in the eternal presence of His glory, we shall be like Him, fully healed, fully fruitful. Then we shall be restored to be God's Delight, like His Beloved Son, who at his baptism was as acclaimed as being well-pleasing to His Father.

Importantly, these fruits listed by the Apostle, which we should produce, are not "us" but "from us"—for they are only to be found fully in Christ Jesus, produced through us by His Holy Spirit indwelling in us. The Apostle Paul, himself, once so proud of being "a Pharisee of the Pharisees" (i.e. "the Reformer of Reformers" of Israel), is himself arrested not by ideology in words, but by the blinding light of the Word, even as he journeyed to Damascus, considered to be the oldest city of trade in the ancient world. So disruptive was his encounter, that the one whom all looked to for leadership "in a religious sense" is now made totally submissive to God's revelation. "Lord," he said, "what do you want me to do?" Later, in his epistles, Paul writes 166 times that becoming a Christian, one must become a new person, now wholly "in Christ."

Many decades ago, I had the great privilege, after attending the Urbana Inter-Varsity Conference, to be encountered in such a way that, like Paul, I have never been the same since. The first night we arrived back from the conference in Winnipeg, where I was a visiting professor, I was awakened early in the morning by a great light at the foot of my bed. Spontaneously, I responded from my heart: "Lord, what do you want me to do?" With no clear answer, I simply waited for six years before I knew what to do. I was to give up my career as a Professor at Oxford, and without promises of any substantial financial support, to start Regent College with a few friends. My pulse-beat every moment since that mystical appearance was like that of the Apostle's witness, before the Roman leader, "So then, King Agrippa, I was not disobedient to the vision from heaven" (Acts 26:19). That has been my heartbeat too, ever since. I became unconscious of "any fruit-bearing," simply of having a new identity "In Christ," and a deepening desire that I would never grow faithless to His heavenly calling on my life. If we do bear any fruit for the Kingdom of God, that is God's assessment as Judge of all the Earth, not ours. His calling to us is to a rootedness in Him, responding to His call for faithfulness, not to our desires, however noble, for success.

Dear friends, as I celebrate my birthday next Monday, surrounded as I will be by my loving family, I can think of no greater joy, no greater blessing, no greater desire of my heart, than that you each push your roots deeper into Christ. If I have desire for having a life "well lived," it is that Christ should bear much fruit for the sake of His Kingdom in the lives of those whom I have been blessed to call my friends. The "well done" for which we all long comes not from our efforts, but from the fruit, borne through Christ, in the lives of others. And so with Francis I pray "make me a channel of your peace...and forbearance, and kindness, and goodness, and self-control and love."

In deepest friendship,

Jim

APPENDIX 1: Letter from the Late Archbishop Nerses Pozapalian

Archbishop Nerses Pozapalian (1937–2009) was in charge of the Armenian Publications in the Holy See of Etechmiadzin, near Yereven, the capital city of Armenia. He had trained all the bishops of the Armenian Church and was the senior candidate to become the Católica (head of the church). However, he felt called of God to step aside and permit his own former student to be elected instead; for he saw his role to be a selfless mentor of his theological alumni. In September 2001, the Armenian Church celebrated 1700 years of existence and with special celebrations including the building of a new cathedral. He took me to examine the new cathedral, juxtaposed on the earlier temple of the pagan Zoroastrian religion that worshiped fire and which had a large cauldron filled with constant burning olive oil. Soon after my visit, he wrote me this letter:

Dear Professor Houston,

I am still remembering your recent visit to the Holy See of Etechmiadzin and the Church of St. Gayne, where I am in charge of the publication of the books of the Holy See. How nice it was to meet you and discuss about many different matters concerning all Christian churches at this time of year after we have celebrated seventeen hundred years of our own church"s history. Together we discussed especially about the Ecumenical Movement, which was by the grace of the Holy Spirit, established in 1948 in Amsterdam, immediately after the Second World War. I expect that the ecumenical movement became a reality because in many countries Christians of good faith have for many centuries been in pursuit of this dream....

In the Armenian communities, for example, from the 12th and the 13th centuries, Saints Nerses Shnorhali and Nerses of Lambron were advocates for Christian Unity and for the establishment of Christian Nurture for minds and in dialogue with diverse Christian communities.

Now the Ecumenical Movement has been established and in Geneva it has its headquarters, but it seems to have become only a selective movement of ecclesiastical and lay readers. But this doesn't race to the bottom where there are ordinary lay people. The twenty first century will have to be a century where there is a relational reformation of the Church, where the Ecumenical spirit and its ideal of unity reaches to the lowest levels of society and can become not only a movement of the upper classes of society, but for the poor and the fringe levels of society; indeed also at the grass-roots!

The present movement of the world is in turmoil, so we Christians have to find new ways and means to restore the desired tranquility to the world, in order that we may give hope and faith to the people of the world. Everywhere secularization dominates over the Churches and our communities. We must then have a special message for ordinary people. I am very happy that I was born into a Christian family. My Mother's godly influence has always been with me, as well as that of my Father and Sisters. Our family was pious. Before eating, before sleeping and before starting on anything, we used to pray. Of course the family environment in which I was brought up has always helped me to devote myself to my Church. God alone knows how much I have been useful.

Hope this letter finds you in good health and Spirit. With God's blessings and with the Love of the Holy Spirit.

I remain faithfully yours,

Archbishop Nerses Pozapalian

APPENDIX 2: Friends of Jim

As one of the many whose life was turned around by meeting Jim Houston, I'm delighted that the Hospital Letters are being published. They stand as Jim's very personal gift to each one of us. They are loving encouragement for living our life in Christ, and food for the journey.

Janet Martin Soskice
Regent 1974

The Apostle Paul wrote thirteen letters that changed the world. Some twenty centuries later, Jim Houston's fifty-three letters from a hospital bed bear witness to the same transforming presence and power of whom Paul wrote. If you wish to live a rooted life, one that abides by streams of flowing water and that bears fruit that will last, then take up these letters and read. Like me, you will find great encouragement for your soul.

Hank Voss
Associate Professor of Christian Ministry at Taylor University
Director of the Sacred Roots Project

Whether you were close to Jim and are reading his letters as one of his intimates, or have picked up this book because of the captivating title and the reputation of the author, you are in for a treat! You will be walking the road of a tremendous intellect, one who was at the same time unusually sensitive to the needs of humanity, and most importantly, one who had a heart for the living and loving God. May we all hear from the Almighty through the ponderings of this consummate teacher, who, even as he turned 100 years old, continued to coach those of us at his feet. Enjoy the feast!

Mark L. Maxwell
President, Prairie College

Jim Houston has always written letters.

My first 'Houston Letter' arrived in early 1968. Jim was newly appointed Principal of the 'Regent Project' to which Marshall Sheppard had earlier recruited me. What followed is history.

A second series of letters followed almost a decade later when I was in Cambridge and the college was wrestling with change. It would end with both Jim and me in new roles, to which neither of us had aspired. Those were difficult days, but what emerged was transformational, not only for the college but for Jim.

Until 1979, Jim was a geographer heading up a theological college. 1978 changed all that, and 'Letters from a Hospital Bed' is the culmination of that change.

Not content with just moving office down the hall, Jim sought, and found, his true calling. Opening his door to students, while exploring a whole range of new topics (e.g., The Christian Mind, The Christian Spirit, Prayer, Spiritual Friendship), Jim responded to a divine calling that, almost half a century later, has seen no letup.

As Betsy and I read Jim's weekly 'letter', I often remarked, 'This is Jim at his absolute best.' Virtually every theme of the past fifty years has re-surfaced in a new, and often fresh, way. With the indispensable collaboration of son Chris, the best wine has been saved for last. Thanks be to God.

Dr. Carl E. Armerding
Colleague and friend 1968-present
Second Principal, Regent College

Friendship with Jim Houston is invariably a double gift, for to have Jim as your friend is to have him also as your spiritual director. An attentive listener and loving practitioner of soul craft, Jim has guided the lives of innumerable students and friends. Neither distance nor age are obstacles to friendship, and in these "Letters from a Hospital Bed," our centenarian friend affectionately offers us his guidance yet again. Jim's friendship and guidance are with us not only in epistolary form but also—as he repeatedly assures us here—in the prayers he kindly offers up for us. May we pass on the gift that our gracious Lord has given us in Jim's love and faithfulness.

Hans Boersma
Saint Benedict Servants of Christ Chair in Ascetical Theology
Nashotah House Theological Seminary, Wisconsin

What a lovely and fitting set of reflections to draw together Jim's century of pastoral and spiritual theology, stretching in almost equal halves before and after the founding of Regent College! There is something deeply captivating in the letter form of these meditations, as a kind of parable of Jim's luminous ministry of friendship and encounter with unnumbered students and colleagues around the world. So much seems to come full circle in this communicative fruit of a long faithfulness. We glimpse in this collection the blessing of a life which, like Simeon's in the Temple, has prevailed to the reward of God's peace and seen the salvation promised and prepared for all nations.

Markus Bockmuehl
Dean Ireland's Professor of the Exegesis of Holy Scripture
Keble College, Oxford

Reading *Letters from a Hospital Bed* by James Houston ("Jim") in his "second wind of life," after having reached the good old age of ninety-nine in 2021, and by his son Chris, his much appreciated amanuensis extraordinaire, I was reminded how blessed I have been to have had Jim as a friend – unworthy as I am -- and as a co-author of three historical commentaries on the Book of Psalms. Jim refers to John Stott as a "rarity"; Jim himself is the "gem of rarest ray serene" in Thomas Gray's *Elegy Written in a Country Churchyard*, but not that poet's "flower born to blush unseen and waste its fragrance on the desert air." Regent students used to joke: 'Ian Rennie, professor of Church History, knows all the evangelicals in Canada; Jim and Rita Houston has had them all to dinner." Steeped in the Patristic fathers—better, in love with them — and rich in reading, lively imagination, and pastoral insights, his letters tug our sleeve by encouraging words and his own example to love God and others more and more and to hate all that is false and pretentious. I know of none that has more height and depth, breadth and width, of love of God and his image than he. Years ago I told Jim that I was diagnosed – misdiagnosed as it turned out – as having Parkinson's disease. Spontaneously, his face writhed in pain, and he blurted out: "Bruce, that's terrible." His spontaneous emotion and honest words comforted me more than the platitudinous bromides offered well-meaningly by others. This is so, because I knew by his responses that he loved me as himself and felt my pain, and by his sharing lightened my emotional burden.

Bruce Waltke
Professor Emeritus of Biblical Studies, Regent College, Vancouver
Distinguished Professor Emeritus of Old
Testament, Knox Theological Seminary

James Houston, an Appreciation:

When I hear his name, my mind has an image of a gentle, warm, wise face, eyes that search out the state of mind that I bring when I come to him, for advice, good counsel, soul wisdom and friendship. Early on, he was one of the visionaries who had come to Canada to found a college for lay Christians in their preparation for Christian ministry.

My first encounter with Jim happened in 1988 when I first came to Regent College to teach a summer school course in keeping a reflective journal as an exercise for developing an ongoing relationship with God. My first husband, Harold, had recently died (cancer), and I was lonely and sad and wondering how I could survive without him, what kind of ongoing life would be possible. I needed to explore my new, frightening identity with a wise, understanding friend because, at that time I didn't see much "light at the end of the tunnel."

So I went to see Jim in his Regent College office, to ask for advice and counsel from this leader who was one of the founding members of Regent. In our conversation I used this image of the dark tunnel as a reflection of my state of mind, and Jim almost immediately rejoined, "When you reach the end of the tunnel you will find yourself on the edge of a cliff. You must throw yourself off the edge of the cliff, and in that sense of abandonment you must trust that God will catch you."

Those were startling words, but offered with such genuine love and wisdom to describe my transfer of the affection and trust I had known with my husband into the love and support I needed to feel with God. Jim was known for this gift of wisdom, entering into the experience of a questioner and using a vivid word picture to illuminate moment of need and a divine response.

Many years later, Jim and I were both invited to speak at a conference for retired professionals. We were invited to discuss the experience of aging, and to share with others what divine wisdom we might have received. What advice did we have to give to others about to retire and leave lives of fruitful employment for … the rest of their lives? The basic question for retirees was "Well, what's next? And where is God in it?"

After our own turn speaking Jim and I were seated together in the front row of the auditorium to hear what practical patterns of life other retirees and professionals were suggesting. I remember our whispered conversation and in particular his final turning to look at me, his face exhibiting his wonderful, warm facial expression. In particular, his loving glance of understanding that said, "We're in this together, and so let's stay in touch and pray for each other." And we have!

One more thing. When I turned ninety-five last month Jim phoned me to wish me a happy birthday. I was deeply moved that old as he was in years, and youthful in spirit, he had not only remembered me, had learned of my birthday, and had reached out across the border to let me know I was remembered with love. Grace and wisdom personified! Of such is the kingdom of God.

Luci Shaw

Notes

1 Corrie ten Boom, *The Hiding Place: the Triumphant True Story of Corrie ten Boom* (New York: Bantam, 1974), 198f.

2 Johnson Oatman, Jr., "Count Your Blessings," (1897).

3 Gregory of Nazianzen, *Oration 38, on the Theophany, or Birthday of Christ,* [unknown edition], V.

4 George Herbert, "Iesu," in *George Herbert, The Complete Works,* ed. John Drury & Victoria Moul (London: Penguin, 2015), 107.

5 Charles Wesley, "Gentle Jesus," (1707-1788).

6 St. Augustine of Hippo, *The Works of Saint Augustine, Letters 1-99,* Volume II/1, trans. Roland Teske, (New York: New City Press, 2001) 224, (ch. 9, para. 17).

7 St. Augustine of Hippo, *The Confessions of Saint Augustine,* ed. Hal M. Helms (Brewster, Mass.: Paraclete Press, 2010) 3.

8 See Appendix 1 for the full text of the Archbishop's letter.

9 See Appendix 1 for the full text of the Archbishop's letter.

10 John of Avila, *Letters of Blessed John of Avila,* trans. Benedictines of Stanbrook (London: Burns & Oates Ltd, 1904) 96 (letter XIV).

11 [Unknown], "Be Thou My Vision," trans. Mary E. Byrne (1905).

12 John Ellerton, "The Day Thou Gavest, Is Ended," (1870).

13 George Herbert, "The Elixir," in *George Herbert, The Complete Works,* ed. John Drury & Victoria Moul (London: Penguin, 2015), 176.

14 George Herbert, "The Elixir," in *George Herbert, The Complete Works,* ed. John Drury & Victoria Moul (London: Penguin, 2015), 176-7.

15 Shirley Erena Murray, "God of Freedom, God of Justice," (1980).

16 Gerard Manley Hopkins, "The Wreck of the Deutschland," in *Gerard Manley Hopkins, the Major Works,* (New York: Oxford University Press, 2009) 118-9.

17 Isaac Watts, "Praise to God for His Goodness and Truth," (1674-1748).

18 © Mark Anderson, used by permission.

19 Isaac Watts, "I Sing th' Almighty Power of God," (1674-1748).

20 St. Augustine of Hippo, *The Confessions,* trans. R. S. Pine-Coffin, (London: Penguin Books, 1961) 243 (ch. 8, para. 8).

21 Charles Wesley, "O Thou Who Camest from Above," (1762).

22 [Citation Unknown]

23 [Citation Unknown]

24 Doris Day, "Whatever Will Be, Will Be (Que Sera, Sera)," Single. Columbia, 1956, Vinyl.

25 St. Augustine of Hippo, *The Confessions of Saint Augustine,* ed. Hal M. Helms (Brewster, Mass.: Paraclete Press, 2010) 195.

26 Nicholas Ferrar, "The Printers to the Reader," in *George Herbert, The Complete Works,* ed. John Drury & Victoria Moul (London: Penguin, 2015), 6.

27 George Herbert, "Mary Magdalene," in *George Herbert, The Complete Works,* ed. John Drury & Victoria Moul (London: Penguin, 2015), 166.

28 Ronald Ritters, "Martin Luther, the Selfless Christian" in *Sources of the Christian Self,* ed. James M. Houston & Jens Zimmerman, (Grand Rapids, Michigan: Eerdmans, 2018) 379-391.

29 Martin Luther, *LW,* 25:135. Quoted in Ronald Ritters, "Martin Luther, the Selfless Christian" in *Sources of the Christian Self,* ed. James M. Houston

& Jens Zimmerman, (Grand Rapids, Michigan: Eerdmans, 2018) 381.

30 John Cassian, *The Conferences* in *Ancient Christian Writers,* trans. Boniface Ramsey, (New York: Newman Press, 1997) 838.

31 Kate B. Wilkinson, "May the Mind of Christ, My Savior," (1925).

32 Richard Crashaw, "The Flaming Heart," in *The English Poems of Richard Crashaw,* ed. Edward Hutton, (London: Methuen & Co., 1901), 122.

33 Laurie Klein, "I Love You, Lord," single, House of Mercy, 1978.

34 Michael Perry, "Heal Me, Hands of Jesus," (1982).

35 John Greenlead Whittier, "Dear Lord and Father of Mankind," (1872).

36 Thomas á Kempis, *The Imitation of Christ,* trans. Robert Jeffery, (London: Penguin Books Ltd., 2013) 147-8.

37 St. Maximus the Confessor, "On The Lord's Prayer," in *The Philokalia, the Complete text (Volume II),* comp. St. Makarios & Nicodemus the Hagiorite, ed. G. E. H. Palmer et al, (London: Faber & Faber, 1990) 288.

38 St. Francis of Assisi, "Make Me a Channel of Your Peace," (1182-1226).

39 C. S. Lewis, *Mere Christianity,* (New York: HarperCollins, 2001) 134.

40 *Origen, Homilies on Luke, Fragments in Luke,* in *The Fathers of the Church, Volume 94,* trans. Joseph Lienhard (Washington, D. C.: The Catholic University of America Press, 1996) 181.

41 *Origen, Homilies on Luke, Fragments in Luke,* in *The Fathers of the Church, Volume 94,* trans. Joseph Lienhard (Washington, D. C.: The Catholic University of America Press, 1996) 182.

42 Oliver Wendell Holmes, "Lord of All Being, Throned Afar," (1848).

43 [Citation Unknown]

44 Marty Haugen, "Healer of Our Every Ill," (1987)

45 John Michael Talbot, "Hesychia Stillness," last modified 2009, https://johnmichaeltalbot.com/hesychia-stillness#:~:text=Those%20who%20wanted%20to%20follow,the%20abundance%20of%20eternal%20life.

46 Catherine von Schlegel, "Be Still, My Soul," trans. Jane Borthwick, (1855).

47 Translation of Spanish Hymn by Rufino Zragoza

48 Rulman Merswin, *Mystical Writings of Rulman Merswin,* ed. Thomas S. Kepler, (Philadelphia, PA: The Westminster Press, 1960) 124-5.

49 Fred Pratt Green, "The Church of Christ in Every Age," (1969).

50 W. P. Mackay, "Revive us Again," (1863, 1867).

51 Brian A. Wren, "Thank You God, for Water, Soil, and Air," (1954).

Printed in the USA
CPSIA information can be obtained
at www.ICGtesting.com
LVHW041107110424
776742LV00003B/9

9 781573 836050